Ceramic Ethnography of The Two Eco-Cultural Zones of Rajasthan

Ceramic Ethnography of The Two Eco-Cultural Zones of Rajasthan

PRITISH CHAUDHURI
Anthropological Survey of India,
Western Regional Centre,
Pratapnagar, Udaipur (Rajasthan)

AAYU

AAYU PUBLICATIONS
New Delhi

Cataloging in Publication Data--DK

Courtesy: D.K. Agencies (P) Ltd. <docinfo@dkagencies.com>

Chaudhuri, Pritish, author.
Ceramic ethnography of the two eco-cultural zones of Rajasthan / Pritish Chaudhuri. -- 1st edn.
pages cm
Includes bibliographical references.
ISBN 9789385161834

1. Pottery--India--Rajasthan. 2. Ethnic art--India--Rajasthan. 3. Human ecology--India--Rajasthan. I. Title.

LCC NK4151.C43 2018 | DDC 738.09544 23

Published by:

AAYU PUBLICATIONS
D-134, Agar Nagar, Prem Nagar-III
New Delhi-110086
Tel: 09910728725, 09654504227
Email: aayupublication@gmail.com
www.aayupublications.com

Ceramic Ethnography of the Two Eco-Cultural Zones of Rajasthan

1st Edn. 2018
ISBN: 978-93-85161-83-4

PRINTED IN INDIA

Printed at: Unitech Graphic Point, Delhi

Dedicated to

My Grandparents

Late Shri Khitish Chaudhuri

and

Late Smt. Sadhana Chaudhuri

PREFACE

First of all, I would like to convey my heartfelt thanks to the Director, Anthropological Survey of India, for providing me this platform to carry out my study in the field of ceramics and for orienting me with new thinking.

I am highly obliged to Dr. A.V. Arakeri (Former Head of office) An.S.I., W.R.C., Udaipur, without whose guidance and official supports it would have been impossible for me to collect and analyse the data in a proper way. Further, I am happy to acknowledge Prof. Lalit Pandey, Dean Faculty of Social Science, B. N. University, Udaipur and Dr. J.S. Kharakwal of Rajasthan Vidyapeeth Deemed University, Udaipur for their co-operation and guidance in the field related collection of data. They all provided me necessary help and suggestion whenever I needed.

My special thanks are also goes to all those potters of Molela and Pokaran, who gave their valuable time to me for the interviews and providing me with rich data. I am very much thankful to all of my colleagues.

CONTENTS

LIST OF MAPS

LIST OF FIGURES

1

INTRODUCTION

About Traditional Knowledge

Traditional Knowledge has acquired the position of a very important and spacious research opportunity throughout the world for mainly two broad reasons. Firstly, as the developing and third world countries of Asia, Africa and Latin America are dissatisfied with their model and role of development which did not possess the rich traditional and practical knowledge of their own people that mould their civilization and culture from the time unmemorable. They merely were ignoring their heritage. Such kind of knowledge contains everything pertaining to their living in their respective ecological and eco-cultural zones and their set up and resource management. Secondly, traditional knowledge showcases the wide range of cultural diversity that formed the basic funda of human existence.

The job of documentation and collection of data on Traditional Knowledge has been facilitated in recent times by the availability of wide variety of theoretical knowledge which derived from rich ethnography all around the globe.

There is no doubt about the fact that India is a hub of Traditional Knowledge. It contains 91 eco-cultural zones which are inhabited by around 4635 distinct ethnic groups and innumerable sub- groups who present almost equally varied traditional knowledge adopted by them which sustain their life.

In the present scenario, the penetration of market forces and globalization of modern technologies has threatened the rich diversity. So this is urgent necessity to record and document such rich tangible and intangible cultural heritage as early as possible before it get completely lost.

Simultaneously many NGO's, Knowledge Commission of India, United Nations Agencies, etc. are undertaking many measures and efforts to document and record such knowledge system in order to protect bio- cultural diversities.

Study on Traditional Knowledge will not only represent the present ocean of knowledge and also an effort to excavate those aspects of Traditional Knowledge which were dead or buried under the soil of time or on the way to vanish. There is always a transition of tradition with the passage of time. New new ideas and elements also joined with the traditional one and sometimes results new innovations.

Definition of Traditional Knowledge: Several definitions of Traditional Knowledge exist in available literature. The World Intellectual Property Organization document (wipo_pub_920.pdf, "http//www.wipo.int/ebookshop") on Traditional Knowledge says "...local communities justly cherish Traditional Knowledge as a part of their very cultural identities. Maintaining the distinct knowledge systems that give rise to Traditional Knowledge can be vital for their future well-being and sustainable development and for their intellectual and cultural vitality. For many communities, it forms part of a holistic world- view and is inseparable from their very ways of life and their cultural values, spiritual beliefs and customary legal system. This means that it is vital to sustain not merely the knowledge but the social and physical environment of which it forms an integral part... No single definition would fully do justice to the diverse forms of knowledge that are held by traditional communities; and no form of legal protection system can replace the complex social and legal system that sustains Traditional Knowledge within the original communities." (p.1-6).

Pottery and Terracotta

The ancestors of potters are giving shape to mud from millions of years. When men became civilized and leading a settled life from that time they started to create objects from clay as because those are easily available in their natural environment especially for storage purposes. The first pottery is said as pinch pot. In a ball of clay the fingers and palm are impressed to create the mouth of the pot. The evidences of making pottery can be derived from the Neolithic era. Those are the coarser pottery generally handmade and sun baked. It contains vessels and bowls which are used to store grain. Often those coarse containers are also used for mixing of colours for their wall paintings. Invention of fire also brings a revolutionary change in their pottery culture. The pre historic pots are generally baked in low temperature which is far better from their earlier sun baked pots. Those potteries are fragile in nature. After the discovery of pottery there is a series of on going revolutionary changes at various ages from time to time in its technique and art forms.

Indus Valley Civilization (2500 B.C.) has shown a revolutionary change in the field of pottery making and terracotta art. It was the age of wheel made pottery. These were characterized by well-burnt black painted red wares. Apart from pottery a huge amount of terracotta figurines and seals and sealing are recovered from the Indus sites of

Harappa and Mohenjodaro. Lots of controversies are there among the scholars about the proper use and purpose of those seals and sealing. Terracotta seals depicting various god and goddesses showcase the religious and social pattern of that ancient civilization. The culture of a society can be derived from its pottery. Potteries of two distinct cultures are varied in nature. That's why in Archaeological excavations we find wide range of potteries and potteries cultures for instances Ochre Colour Pottery, Painted Grey Ware, Northern Black Polished Ware, Black and Red Ware, Kayatha Ware, etc. Gupta period (300 A.D. to 600 A.D.) showed us a new series of clay art e.g. painted pottery, designs made by impression, stamping on the vessels, moulded clay articles, decorative tiles and plaques, etc.

The medieval period (12th cent. A.D.) of India is well known for the phase of glazed pottery. During the time of Muslim invasion, the Muslim rulers also bring this Persian art in India.

The word "terra- cotta" means baked clay. Side by side with pottery making terracotta art also flourished in India. Terracotta art is generally red or biscuit colour in nature. Terracotta idols also have a ritualistic value associated with it. This is the fact that the varieties of terracotta votives are used in many auspicious occasions. Terracotta art in India is regarded as mystical because it assemble the five elements i.e. air, fire, water, earth and ether.

From the above mentioned discussion it is clear that playing with clay and water in order to give a definite shape is the oldest craft known to human culture. This tradition is still present in India as well as around the globe. Lots of traditional knowledge is involved with this craft. So this project is launched to find out those hidden treasures. Today lots of small scale and cottage industries are working together to keep this tradition alive. In rural India still now we can see the picture of women carrying water pots on their head fetching water from one village to another. In every house of Indian villages water is stored earthen pots to keep the water cool and pure. In many rituals also water is offered to the deities in pitcher or kalash. The community engaged with this profession is known as potter. The further description of this community will be describe in the chapter of 'About the Community' in this report.

As from the preliminary information it is known that much research work has not yet carried out on the pottery of Rajasthan despite this state consists of wide varieties of pottery culture which has to be explored. There is a wide scope for researcher in this particular field. The exploration on this research area would provide a platform for future research scholar to reconstruct the history and development of human culture from Archaeological, Historical and Ethnographical point of view based on pottery. This research will also enhance our knowledge about many tangible and intangible traditional knowledge of our rural India which is passing on from one generation to another. The art of pottery making is an ancient tradition and a study on this, that how the present pot making community are still maintaining this tradition without being affected by this modern influence. The roots of our present civilization and culture lay down in the past; hence the ethnographical study on pottery culture will provide us an in-depth idea about our golden art and technology. This study will also make us aware about the present status of the pottery tradition, the communities involved with this profession directly or indirectly, their inter relationship and the social phenomenon. On the basis of this report we can make further measures to promote and conserve this rich art and craft in which many of the communities depend.

Objectives of the Study

1. To study the traditional knowledge of the art and art forms.
2. In-depth study of various forms of pottery, their techniques of manufacturing pottery and other terracotta objects.
3. To study the various forms of rich art and craft in the two eco-cultural zones of Rajasthan which depicts the identity of the community and cultural and geographical area they belong to.
4. The socio-economic and the ritual significance of the products and the present changes.

Methodology

Before undertaking the field work, first of all I made myself well equipped with the information related to origin, history and other issues of that particular area and community and their traditional knowledge. Library work was also done from time to time. Visiting some of the important libraries which are situated in Rajasthan, Delhi and Kolkata works out to be fruitful to enhance my knowledge in this particular field. Discussions with the eminent scholars who has already worked in this field turned out to be fruitful. Reconnoitre tour was undertaken to select the suitable villages and the area for the study. Interviews with the knowledgeable and elderly persons of the villages was also conducted. Participation in the socio-ritual functions, festivals and other ceremonies gives me an insight views regarding the subject matter of the study.

Before proceeding on field a list of questionnaires and schedules was prepared in order to collect data on pottery and terracotta techniques, art forms, various activities related with pottery and the life style and population of present potter's community. Special care was also taken for the collection of both qualitative and quantitative data. All the data collected are thus crossed checked by personal interviews and with available records. Though much not work has been done in this field as per my knowledge I collected. Office supplied me camera to take the photographs and other stationary articles like notepad, pen, pencil, eraser, scale, board files, etc. which are required in the field. After the completion of the field work the collected data are all analysed and processed and presented in this book.

Work Plan and Field Limitations

The state of Rajasthan is broadly divided into two eco-cultural zones Mewar and Marwar. So it was decided to cover one area for study from each region. The field area was selected on the basis of concentration of potters with their technological variations, soil type, social structure, ethnic differences and so on. In this respect district gazetteers, census report, previous reports and other available literatures are studied. In this project three months field work was conducted and hence accordingly work plan was distributed in the following phases:

1: Collecting literature from secondary sources, Gazetteers, etc.

2 : Preparation of schedules and guidelines for the study

3 : Conducting field work and collection of data

4 : Analysis of data

5 : Writing of report.

The first phase of field work was conducted in the month of June 2011 at Molela (Rajsamand district) for fifteen days as pilot survey. Next, one and half month field work was conducted in the same field in the month of August-September 2011. At last, final phase of field work was conducted in January 2012 for one month period. The field area was at Pokaran (Jaisalmer district). Hence, Molela was selected from Mewar region and Pokaran from Marwar region. Before the selection of the above mentioned field areas, Nathdwara, Bagol, Parawal, Khamnor (Rajsamand district), Jaisalmer, Kanoi (Jaisalmer district) and Jodhpur was also survayed. The detail information about the field is mentioned in the following chapter.

The initial problem I faced is undertaking a field work in a completely new state. It took time for me to accustom with the environment, culture, people and climate. Further the language is being a big factor to carry out the field study smoothly. The selection of the field area and study units was an unmanageable job because of the communication gap. It was quite a difficult task to dig out the entire information within the specific time. Particularly in the field the rapport establishment was quite a challenging task. There are some people who create problems while undertaking the field work. So dealing with such people and managing the informant was a time consuming process. Apart from all these factors, the distance among the field areas of my study and the lack of proper transport was also remain factors which can also be included in my field limitations.

Organization of Data

By going carefully through the report one can get the idea that how the various factors carrying out the trend of pottery and terracotta art in the two eco-cultural zones of Rajasthan. Description of the field along with map is also provided in this book. The two different eco-cultural zones of Rajasthan are different is all respect. Hence they varied in soil type, climatic condition, natural environment and so on which affects their culture, food habits and the pottery type and techniques.

Next comes about the methods, tools and techniques which the potters generally apply for manufacturing their products. The chapter of Tools and implements will describe about the names of various tools and its probable function of both the field areas. The description of final products they sell to the market area also mentioned. The uses of those products in the social and religious life give an idea about the importance of pottery in our Indian culture. Techniques also include the firing methods, percentage of heat they apply, etc. Then comes the art forms and designs such as painting, engraving, embossing, graphite and others which show cases the art form of each region. The information about the various organization who played vital role for the promotion of this art and craft is equally valuable. Side by side photographs are also provided to supplement the data.

This study speaks about the community (potters) which is engaged with this profession of both the field (Molela, and Pokaran) and the history and background about their origin. Further description is provided about their number of families, population, sex composition, marital status, literacy rate and occupation in table format. The interrelation with the other communities which mould their social, economical, political, etc. life is also mentioned herewith.

2

ABOUT THE FIELD

The state of Rajasthan is situated in the north- western part of India. It is situated in between 23° 3'N to 30° 12'N latitude and 69° 30'E to 78° 17'E longitude. The total area of Rajasthan is 3, 42,239 sq.km. This is the largest state of India according to its area and covers the 10 % portion of total India. Its stretches about 826 km from north to south and 870 km towards east- west direction.

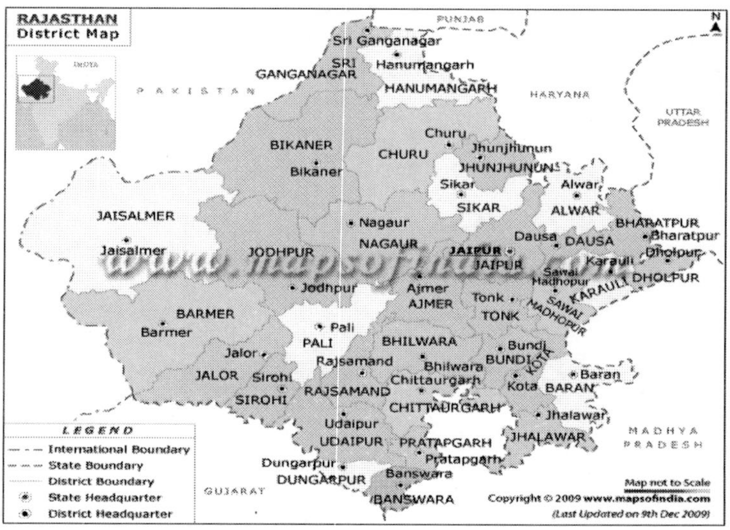

MAP No. 1 – District Map of Rajasthan

The state which we now know by the name of 'Rajasthan' was neither a political unit nor geographical unit before the independence. From the ancient time onwards the different regions were came to known by different names from time to time.

This state was divided into many Rajput kingdoms. The Mughal historians describe 'Rajput' as 'Rajputan' in plural form. Following this term later the British came to call this state as 'Rajputana'. Col. James Todd first described this state by mentioning the name 'Rajasthan' in his book "Annels and Antiquities of Rajasthan".

"Rajasthan is the collective and classical denomination of that portion of India which is the abode of princes. In the familiar dialects of these countries it is termed Rajwada, but by the more refined Raethana Corrupted to Rajputana, the common designation among the British to denote the Rajput- principalities- Todd, Annels, P 1.

According to 2001 census the total population of Rajasthan is 5, 64, 73, 122. This colourful state with its rich cultural heritage is best shoots for cultural exploration and research. The entire state is divided into five eco-cultural zones viz. Mewar, Marwar, Harauti, Sekhawati and Bagdi. Rajasthan is having total 32 districts.

Geographically speaking Rajasthan is divided into four parts:

1. North- West desert region.
2. Central Aravalli part.
3. Eastern plain land.
4. South- East plateau region.

For my study I choose each field area from two different districts situated in two different ecological zones which is already been mentioned earlier. In the following report writing, first of all I will give a brief description about the districts as my unit of study and then the field area or the village where I conducted my field work. The descriptions are as follows:

Rajsamand

The name of this district comes from the name of the artificial lake 'Rajsamudra' which is situated in this region. Rajsamand is located at 73° 28'- 74° 18' E longitude and 24° 26'- 26° 01' N latitude. The total area is 4, 768 sq.km. According to the 2001 census the total population of Rajsamand is 9, 86, 269. Located just about 50 km in the northern direction of Udaipur. It is connected by nearby railway station Mawli which is about 22 km from Nathdwara. Also well connected by road ways. Nearby airport is situated at Udaipur.

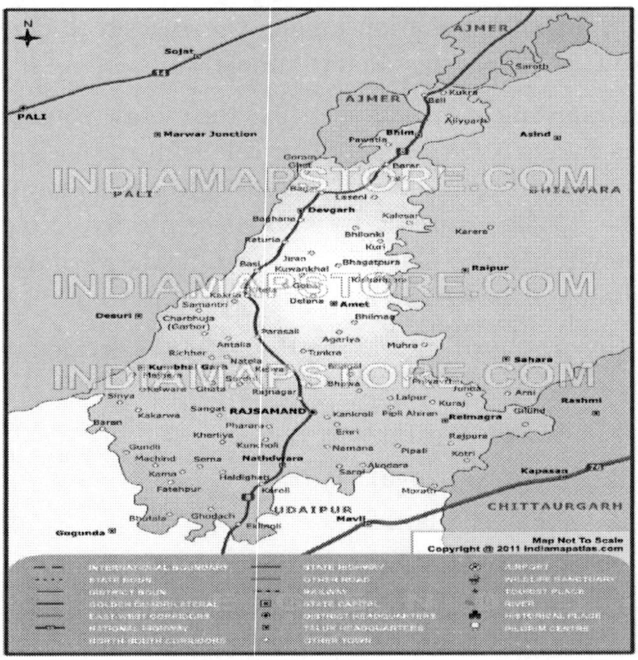

MAP No. 2 – Rajsamand District Map

Molela

The village 'Molela' is situated within Rajsamand district and comes under the Nathdwara Tehsil and Khamnor Panchayat Samiti. This small village is located about 60 km distance towards the northern direction from Udaipur. Molela is famous for its rich terracotta art. Nearby town is Nathdwara which is 10 km away from the village. This old village is situated on the bank of River Banas which harnessed the 4000 years old Ahar/ Banas Culture. The total area of Molela is 1294 hector. Molela is surrounded by seven villages. Village Parawal is situated in east and Kosiwada and khedi is situated in the west of Molela. In the same manner village Usarwas and Khedliya surrounded the northern part of Molela and border of village Khamnor and Sarsunia touches the southern region of Molela.

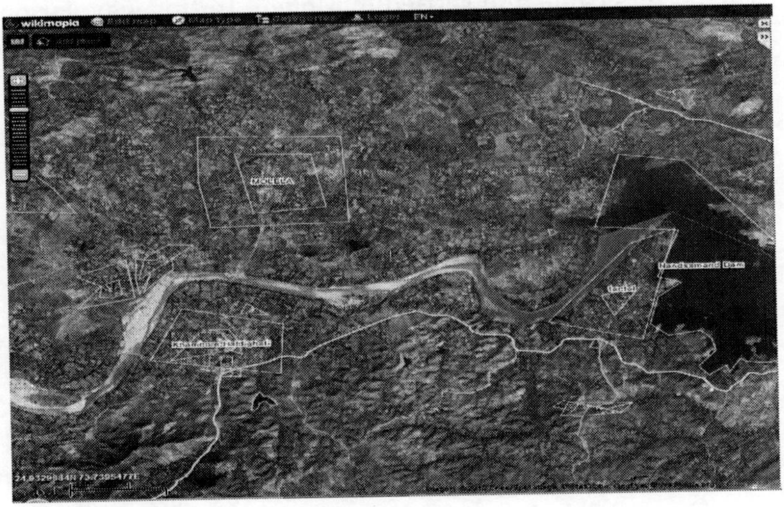

MAP No. 3 – Satellite Picture of Village Molela

Although 'Molela' is an old village but its name is not that much old. In ancient time this village is known by the name of 'Juna Nathdwara'. Verbally it is said that in the place of

Juna Nathdwara there was a village named 'Jaigarh'. After the destruction of Jaigarh the later settlement which came to originated was came to be known by the name of 'Molela'.

There is a historical story behind the origin of this village. The village person tells the story that 'Molya Odhe' was the first people who came in Molela and settled. From this 'Molya Odhe' the name of 'Molela' occurs. They came and settled in Molela long before the battle of Haldighati, the great battle which was fought in between MaharanaPratap and the Mughals. The Mughal army also camped in Molela. The Molya Odhe are generally attached with the work of digging wells, transportation work, building and painting of fort's walls and other masonry related works. They are the labourers. After them the agricultural community came. Later they came to be known as 'Jatiya Mali'. Then the potters came and settled in Molela. In this way various people belonging to various communities came and settled from time to time.

According to the Molela Village Panchayat Official record, the total population of the village is 4367. Out of which:-

- Total no. Of families in Gram Panchayat are 1125.
- No. of SC families are 173.
- No. of ST families are 22.
- No. of OBC families are 547.
- No. of BPL families are 383.

One of the interesting features is that the village consists of many bhagals (community based colonies). The names of the bhagals are as follows:

- Ranbawdi Bhil kiBasti.
- UdawattokiBhagal.

- GairiyokiBhagal.
- KalbeliaBasti.
- BhopakiBhagal.
- MundawalaJatiyaBasti.
- Mundawala Mali Basti.
- KhedakiBhagal.
- OvrikiBhagal.
- BrahmanokiBhagal.
- DojmakiBhagal.
- The central village Molela.

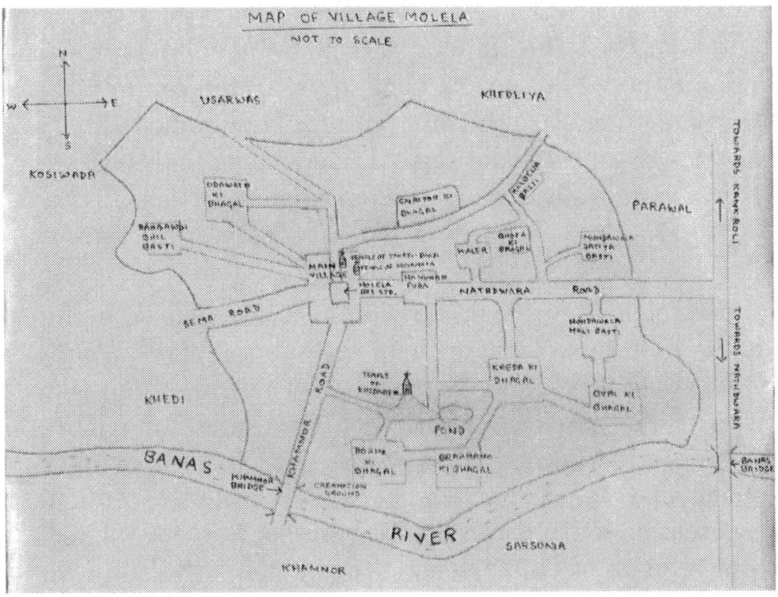

MAP No. 4 – Village Molela

The centre of the main village is resided by the potter's families. Apart from potters the village is also resided by

Jain, Rajputs, Sutars, Gadoliya Lohar and many other communities. From the preliminary information it is noted that the Rajputs form the majority group. The 'bhagals' are all scattered and situated at distance place from one another. They are connected with each other by kaccha roads. During the time of rain it became miserable to move from one 'bhagal' to another through these kaccha roads. The 'bhagals' are mainly inhabited by the said specified communities the 'bhagal' belong. So, from the above mentioned discussion it is clear that the village 'Molela' is a multi- ethnic village.

There is also a doubt about the original settlers of Molela.Regarding this there are two opposite theories. One set of people opines that, the tribes like 'Ranbawdi Bhil', Sahariya, etc. are the original settlers. They are staying in this region from the time of unmemorable. One the other hand, another set of people holds that, all the communities of the said village are the immigrants. They came to Molela from time to time and get settled. They make their own way of living and finally became the permanent settler.

Shrines

In Molela there are many small shrines for worship. But the prominent among them are the temple of 'Takaji-Baoji', 'Khedadevi' and 'Sriyamata'. They are the ethnic deities. Some person says that 'Takaji' and 'Dharmaraj' are the same, whereas other people say that 'Takaji' is the 'Nagadeva'. One point is to be noted that Khedadevi temple is located on the hill top of the village. The word 'kheda' means 'a piece of land'. Hence, Khedadevi is the deity who owned the land of Molela. That's why her temple is placed on the top most part of the village, there is a belief that from the top she use to look after the village and protect the village and its people from all type of dangers. These ethnic deities were worshiped along with the other pantheons of Hindu mainstream.

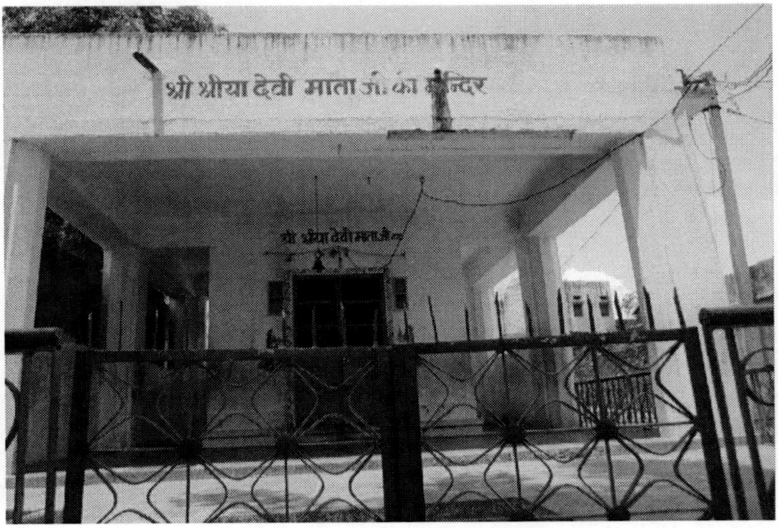

Fig. 1.1 Sriyamata Temple

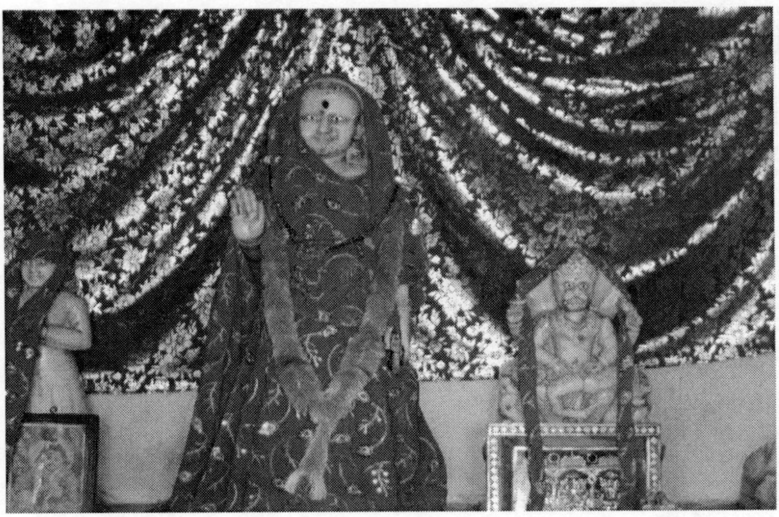

Fig. 1.2 Sriyamata idol

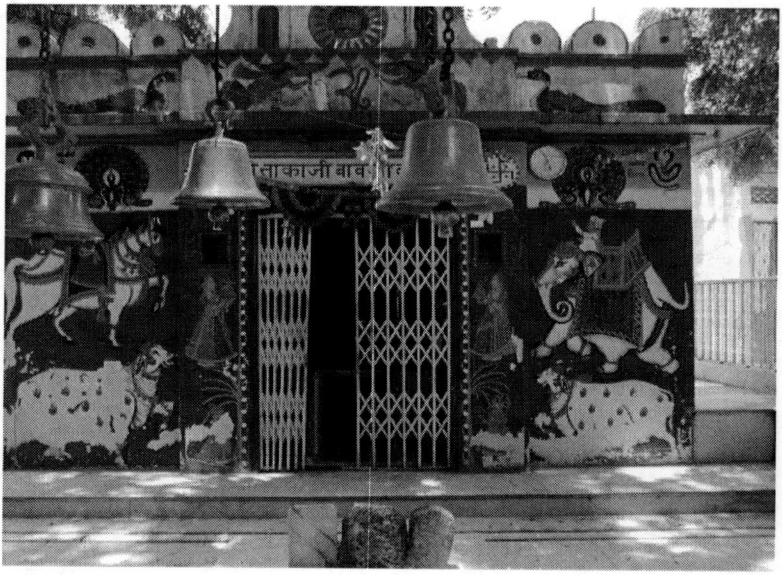

Fig. 1.3 Takaji Baoji Temple

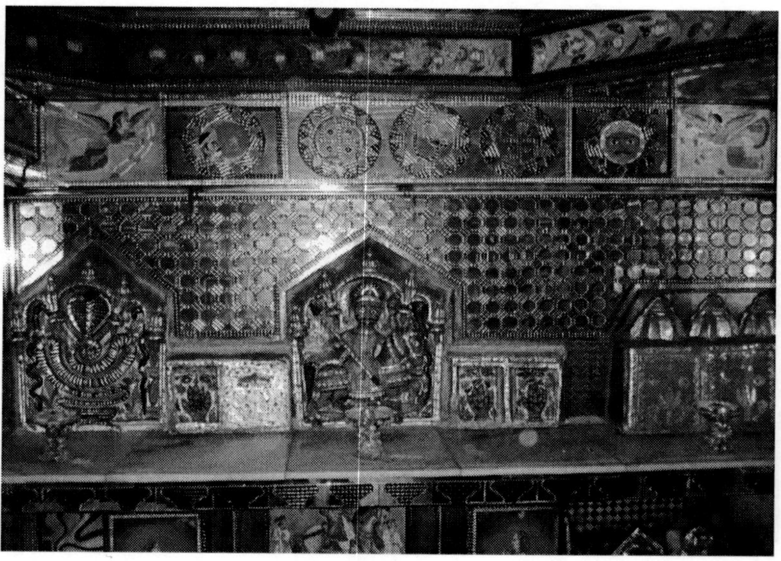

Fig. 1.4 Idols of Takaji- Baoji

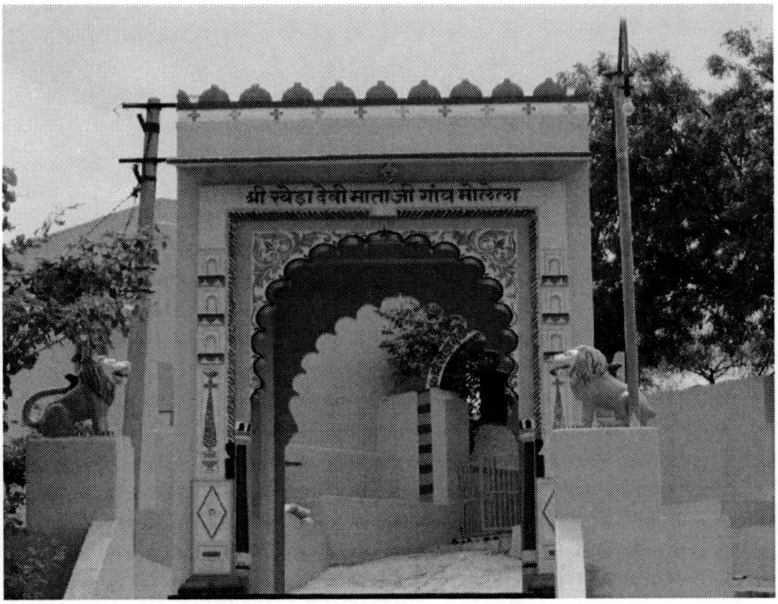

Fig. 1.5 Temple of Kheda Devi

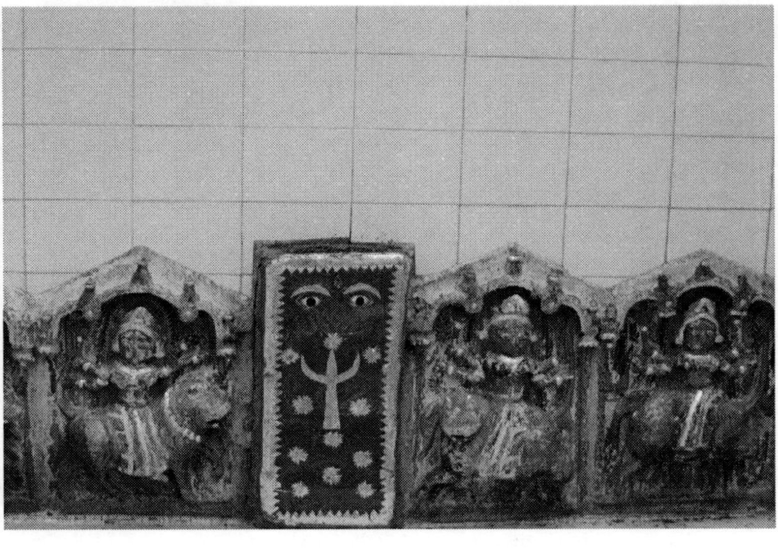

Fig. 1.6 Idol of Kheda Devi

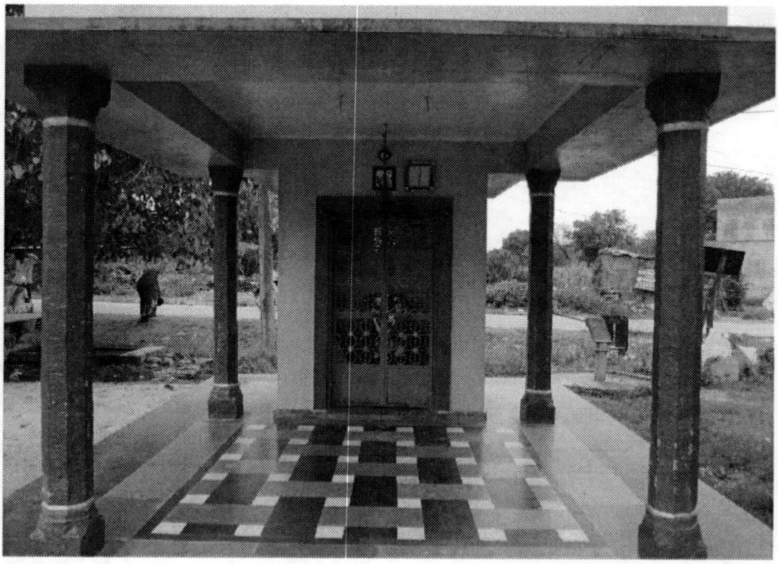

Fig. 1.7 Hanuman Temple

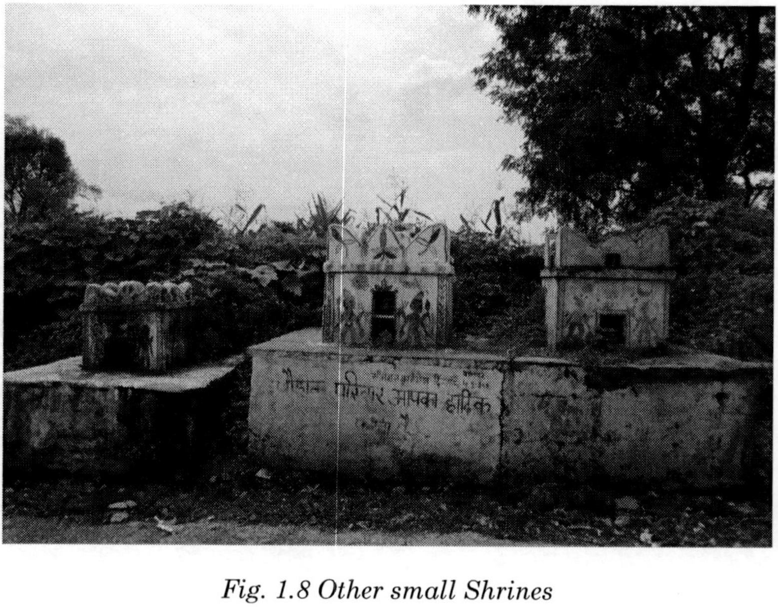

Fig. 1.8 Other small Shrines

Fairs and Festivals

As we all know that, Holi, Ganesh Chathurthi, Dusheera, Diwali, etc. are the main festivals which are celebrated all over India. Apart from these major festivals the people of Molela also celebrate their regional festivals with all pomps. Those are also regarded as the main festival of that village. 'Gavri' festival is organised during 'Raksha Bandhan'. This is one of the main festivals.

The 'Utsav' of 'Dharmaraj' is celebrated after the 'Punam' (full moon) in the rainy season according to the 'Badwi' month of Hindu calendar once in a year in the two major temples of Molela for two consecutive days i.e. in the temple of 'Takaji- Baoji' and 'Kheda Devi' . This festival is known by the name of 'Badwi Chhat'. The season of monsoon is the season of fertility and of great hope. That's why they worship those deities in order to please them so that the deities would shower their blessings on them.

Jaisalmer

Jaisalmer district is situated in the very heart of Thar desert in the western most part of Rajasthan. It is located in between 26° 01' to 28° 02'N latitude and 69° 29' to 72° 20'E longitude. Its north- west portion shares the international border with Pakistan. The name of the district head quarter 'Jaisalmer' originates from the combination of two words 'Jaisal' and 'Meru'. The state of 'Jaisal' was established by Rao Jaisala and 'Meru' was the fort build by him. In this way the meaning of 'Jaisalmer' is "the fort of RaoJaisala". Before the formation of this district in 1949, the state of Jaisalmer was divided into 18 small kingdoms.

Presently the total area of Jaisalmer is 38, 401 sq.km. According to 2001 census the total population of this district was 5,07, 999. Inspite of being a biggest district of Rajasthan its population is low as compared with the other districts of Rajasthan.

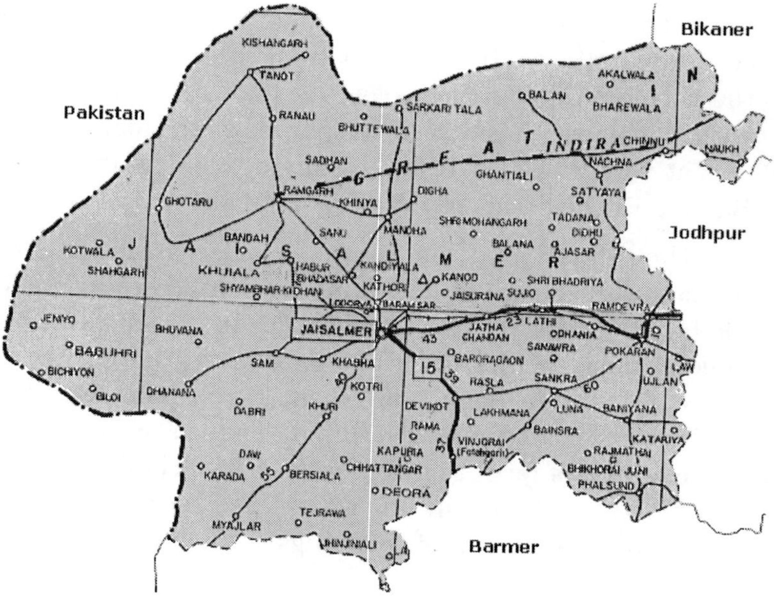

MAP No. 5 – Jaisalmer District Map

Pokaran

Pokaran is situated about 105 km away from the District Head Quarter town of Jaisalmer. Pokaran is located at 26.92° N 71.92° E. The meaning of 'Pokaran' is "the land of five mirages". The entire region is surrounded by sandy and five salt ranges locally known as 'Rann'. According to the 2001 census the total population was 19,186. It is well connected with the road ways both Jodhpur to Jaisalmer and Bikaner to Jaisalmer. Pokaran is famous for its pottery. The town of Pokaran comes under the Pokaran Tehsil and Pokaran Municipality.

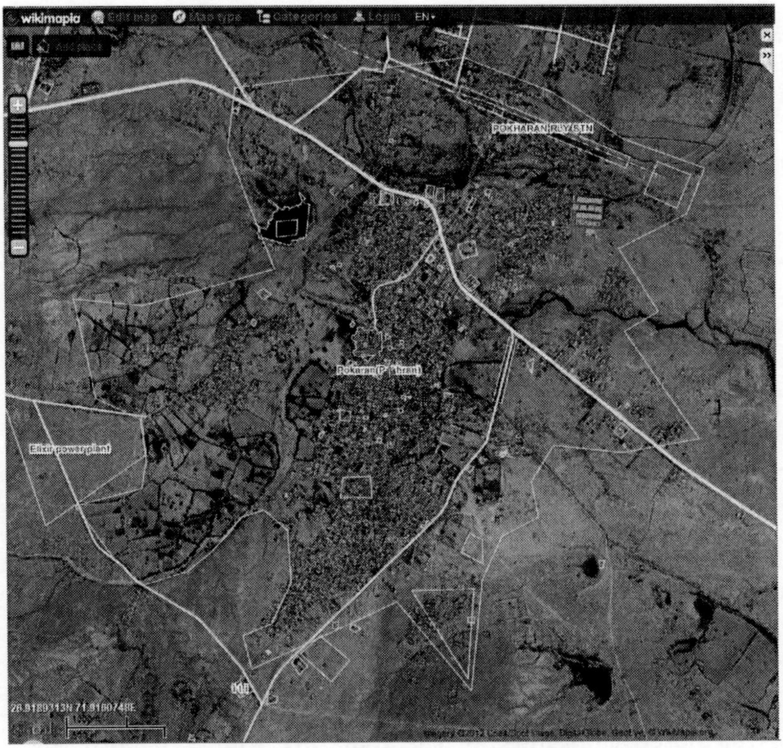

MAP No .6 – Satellite Picture of Pokaran

3

TRADITIONAL TOOLS OF POTTERS

Artisans and the tools are always inseparable with each other. An artisan without his tool is unbelievable. It is considered as part of their body. Here in this chapter the names of all traditional and modern tools of potters are mentioned with its proper function. It gives detail information about all the tools on the basis of the data collected from both the field (Molela and Pokaran). During the course of field work, it was noted that most of the tools are found in both the regions but there are certain tools which are region specific. Along with the name of the tools, the name of the finding area is also mentioned.

The traditional tools of potters are as follows:

Wheel or 'Chak': The first and foremost tool of a potter is 'chak'. 'Chak' or 'wheel' shows the identity of potter. The potter's wheel in India can be divided into two major groups, namely, 'single- wheel' and 'double- wheel'. 'Single wheel' is turned by hand. It is further divided into two sub groups, namely, 'pivoted- wheel' and 'socketed- wheel'. These sub groups can also be classified into two sections: 'spoked-wheel' and 'block- wheel'. (Saraswati and Behura, 1966).

But in the both of my field area I found 'block- wheel'. The wheels are either pivoted or run by baring system (Fig. 2.2). In pivoted- wheel system the entire wheel is balanced on a single nail which is fixed in the ground with concrete. The nail is made up of iron and its size is about 4-5 cm. In Molela, the wheel found is made up of cement with iron coils supporting the structure from inside and in Pokaran, the wheels are generally made up of Plaster of Paris which is mixed with sack and jute ropes. To give support to the structure thin iron rods are there insidewhich were further wrapped with jute sack ropes.

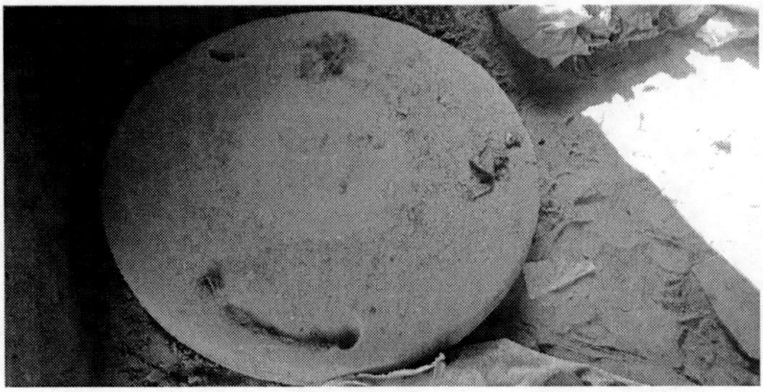

Fig. 2.1, Traditional Wheel, Pokaran

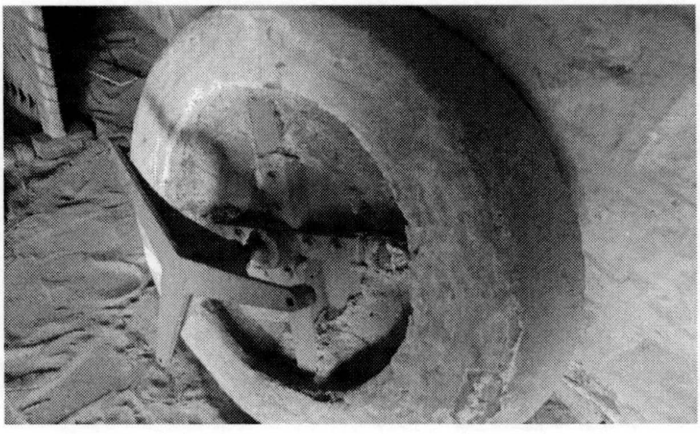

Fig. 2.2, Baring Wheel, Pokaran

The diameter of the wheel varies from approx 60- 70 cm and the thickness varies from 6-7 cm. The main function of the wheel to give regular shape to a clay ball in the form of a pottery.

Stick or 'Lakdi' (Fig. 2.3): Turning stick or 'lakdi' is generally made out of bamboo. Its size may vary from 100 to 130 cm. One end of this tool is made slightly pointed so that it can be fixed into the hole made on the wheel while turning. 'Lakdi' is used for turning the wheel (Fig. 2.4).

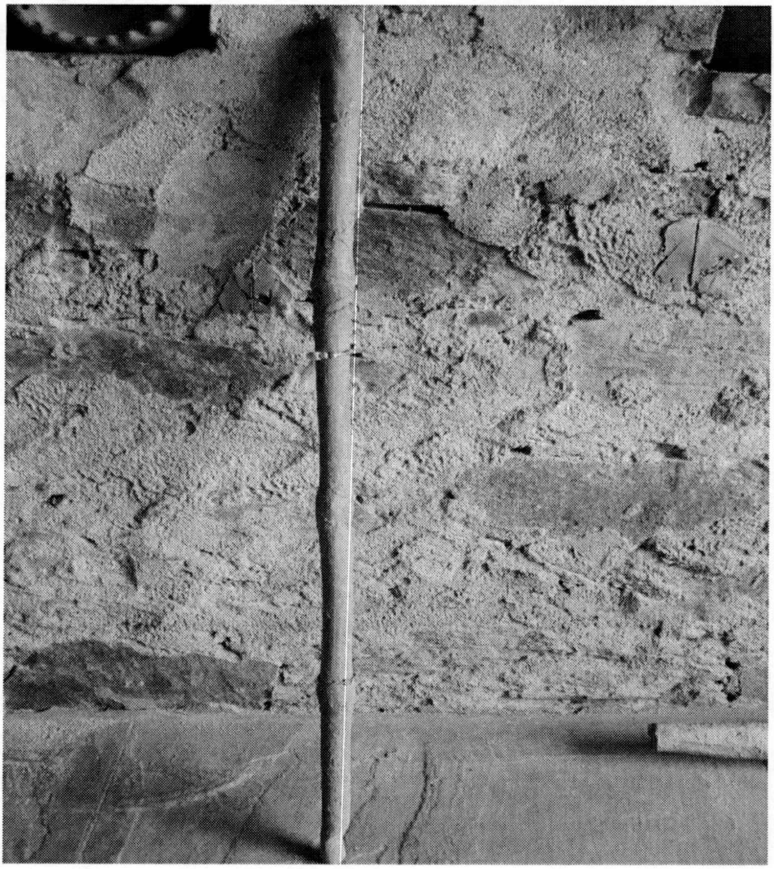

Fig. 2.3 Lakdi

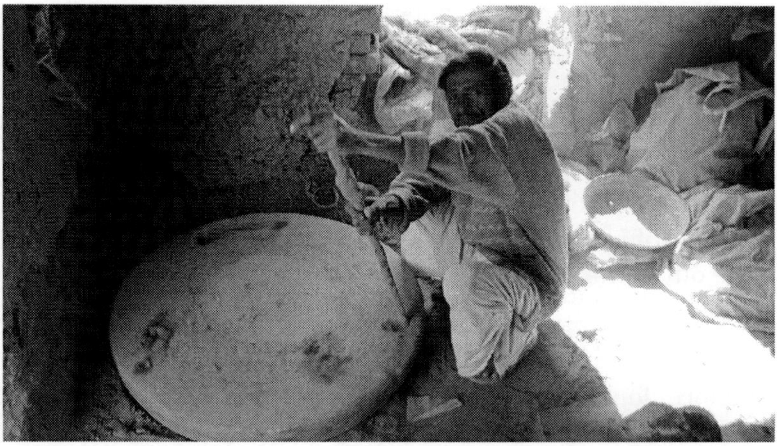

Fig. 2.4, A potter using 'Lakdi' for turning the wheel

Wodden Club or 'Mokhdi': This wooden tool (Fig. 2.5) is specially designed to ram the soil before the treatment and soil preparation. Traditionally it is known as 'Mokhdi'.

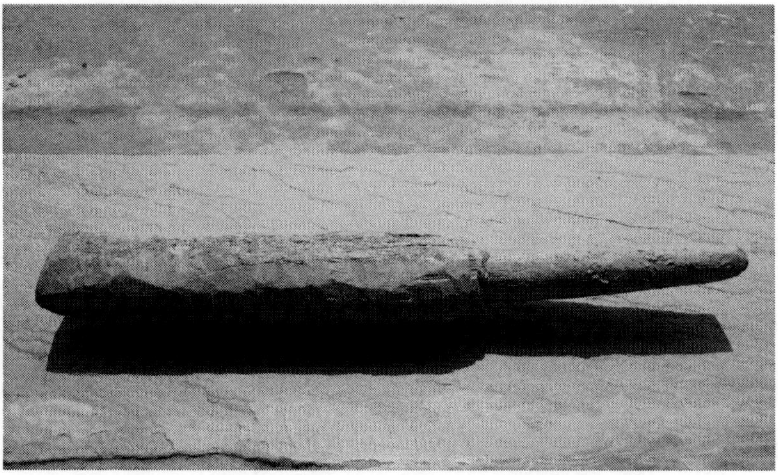

Fig. 2.5 'Mokhdi'

Digging Tools: Tools such as spade and shovels are use to dig out the soil.

Beater or 'Thapa': This tool is made up of wood (Fig. 2.6). Traditionally known 'Thapa' is generally made with hard but light wood such as 'Seesam', 'Robusta', 'Peepal', etc. It is use for enlarging and smoothening the pot after removing from the chak (Fig. 2.7). Its function is equally suitable for both wheel made and hand made pottery. While in case of joining two parts of a pottery it is use for tapering the outer wall (Fig. 2.8).

Every potter posses different sizes and weights of beater. A beater has two parts, handle and the body. The general length of a beater is 30 cm. The length of the handle vary from 12 to 15 cm and the breath of the working body is 12 cm. The thickness is about 2.5 cm. A light beater weights about 250 to 300 grams. Usually the beater has two working surfaces.

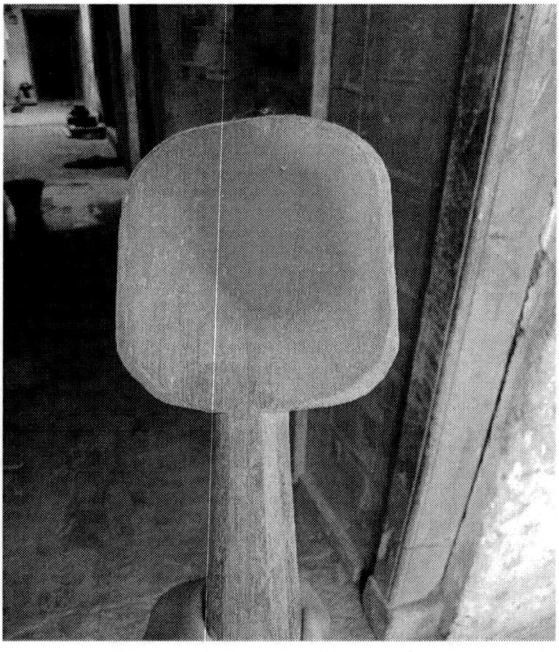

Fig. 2.6, Beater or 'Thapa'

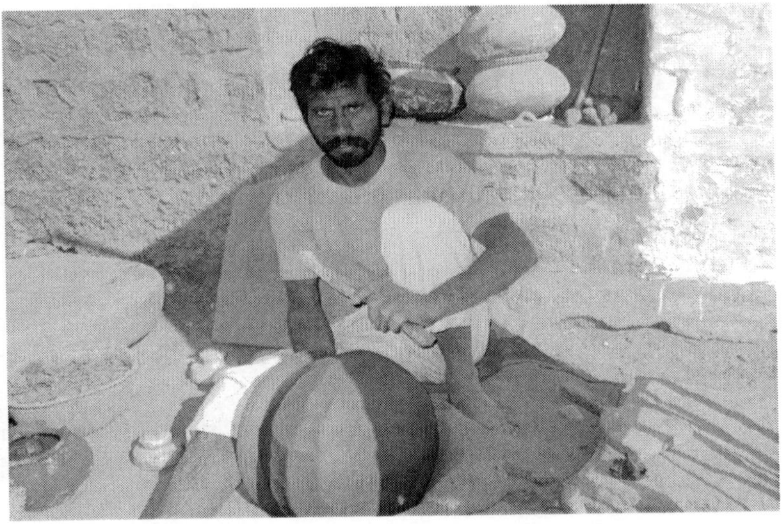

Fig. 2.7, A Pokaran potter enlarging the pot

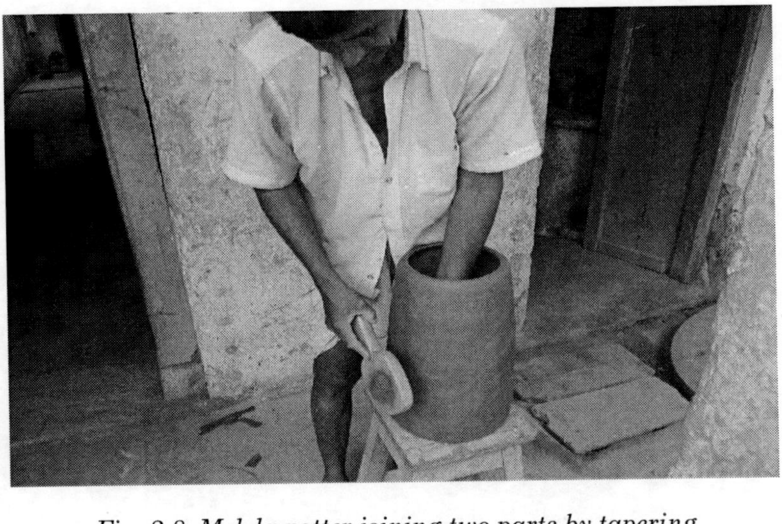

Fig. 2.8, Molela potter joining two parts by tapering

Anvil or 'Pindi' (Fig. 2.9): An anvil traditionally called 'Pindi' by the potters of Molela and Pokaran is made up of clay or stone. Potters generally made this implement by their own but 'Pindi' made up of stone is made by the stone cutters. Stone used is marble granite which is widely used. 'Stone Pindi' became quite popular in Rajasthan because it lasts long and marble is easily available in Rajasthan. 'Pindi' is consisting of a grip and a working surface. The working surface is both flat and slightly convex. Flat surface 'Pindi' is used by Molela potters for smoothening their terracotta plaque plates (Fig. 2. 10) and convex 'Pindi' is used by Pokaran potters for enlarging and shaping their pots. It gives support to the inner wall while beating with a beater.(Fig. 2.11).

The diameter of the working surface varies from 5 cm, 7 cm, 10 cm and even 13 cm. And the length of the 'Pindi' also varies according to the size of its diameter (Fig. 2. 12)

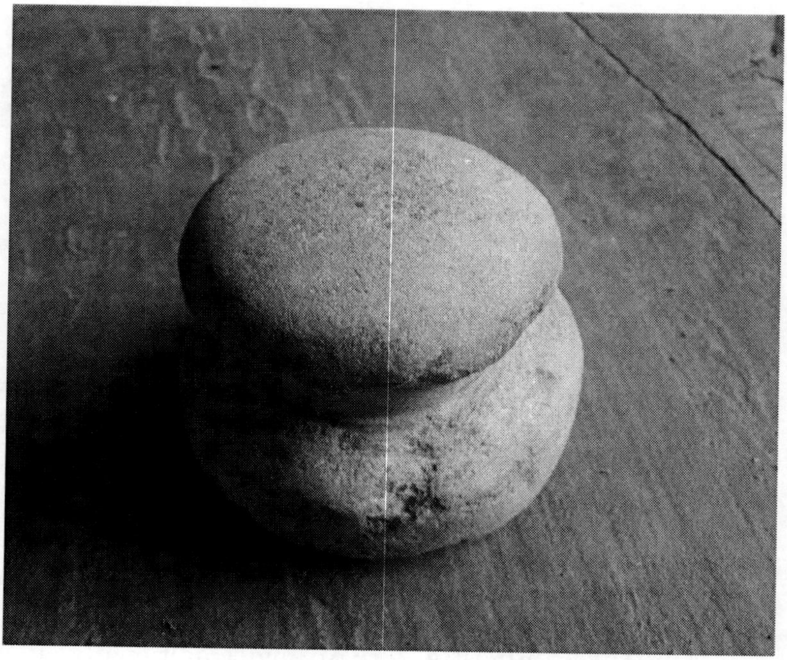

Fig. 2.9, Anvil of 'Pindi'

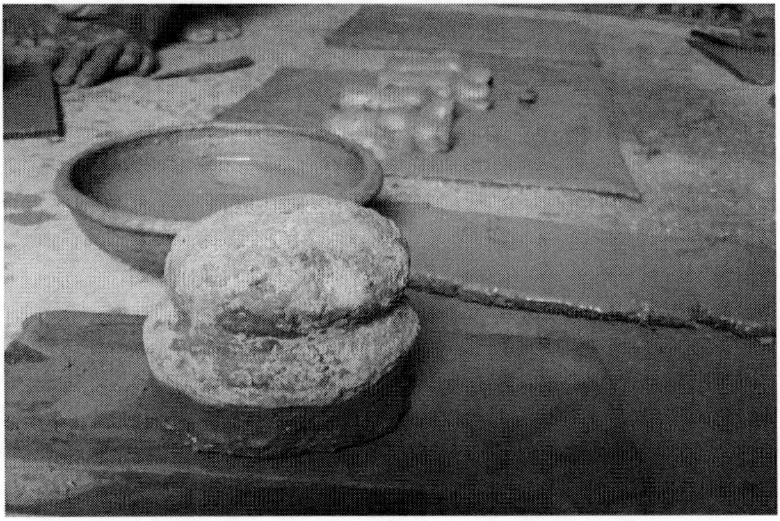

Fig. 2.10, 'Pindi' using for smoothening the plate, Molela

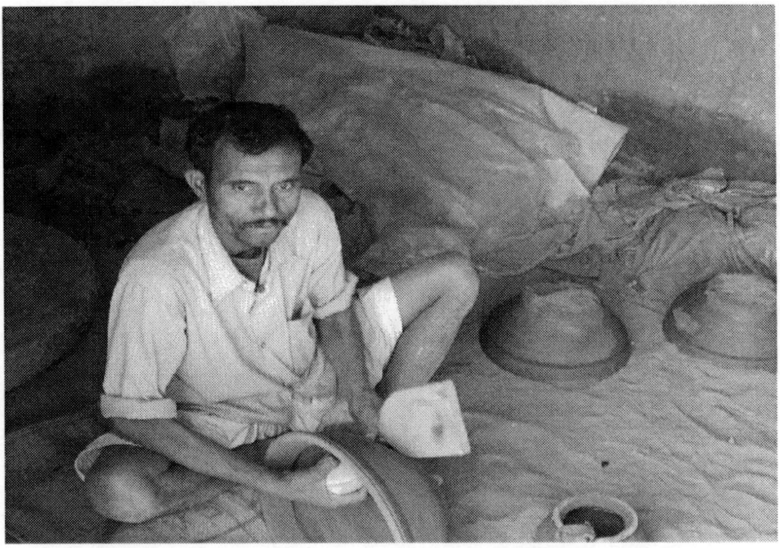

Fig. 2.11, 'Pindi' supporting the inner wall of the pot while beating, Pokaran

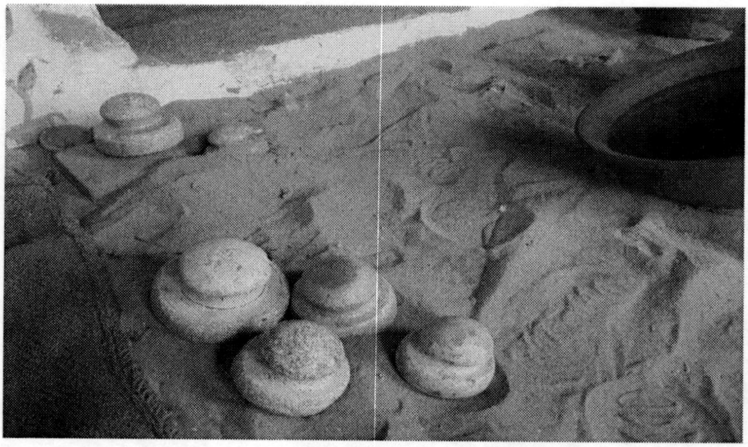

Fig. 2.12. 'Pindi' of various sizes from Pokaran

Wooden Block or 'Patiya': This tool is particularly use in 'Molela'. Locally it is known as 'Patiya'. It is actually a block of wood which constitute the same function of an 'Anvil' or so called 'Pindi'. It is also often use as a substitute of 'Pindi'. See Fig. 2.13.

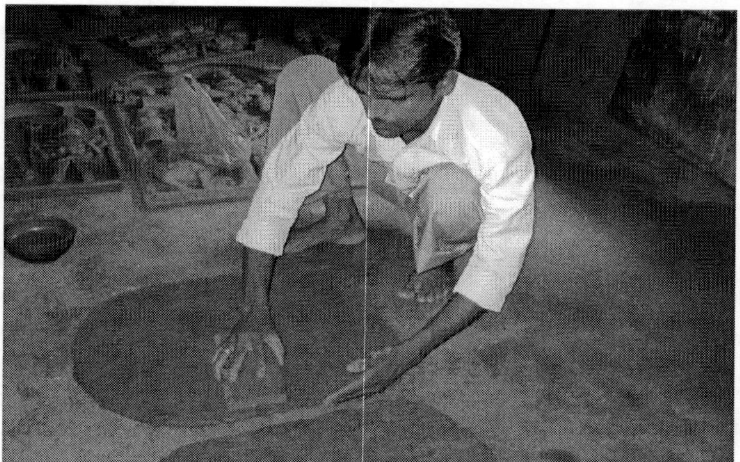

Fig. 2.13, Molela potter using 'Patiya'

Challni: 'Challni' is use to remove the lumps from the soil. It acts as a filter. This is made up of tin or iron. See Fig. 2.14.

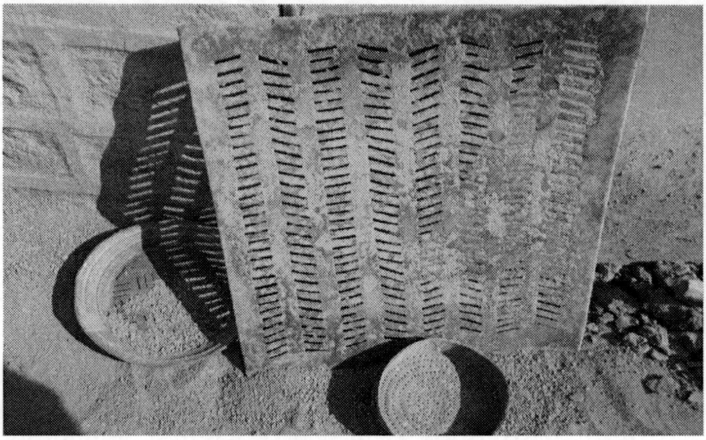

Fig. 2.14, Challni

Scraper or 'Khurpa' (Fig. 2.15): This tool is made up of iron used for scrap out the unwanted clay from the half dried pot. It is also used for thinning the outer wall of the pot (Fig. 2.16). The outer diameter of this tool is 8.5 cm and the inner diameter is 6.5 cm recorded from Pokaran.

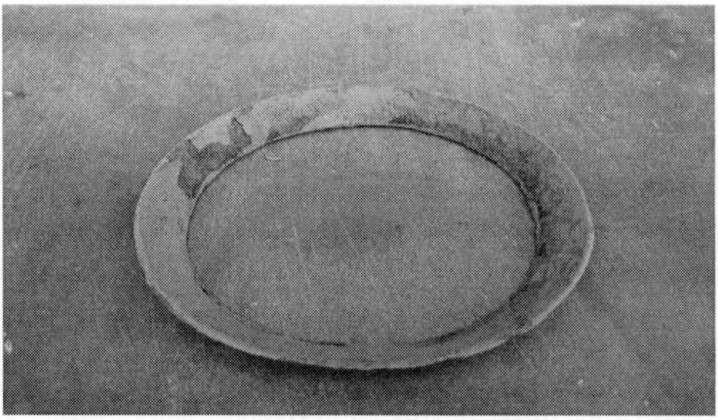

Fig. 2.15, Scraper or 'Khurpa'

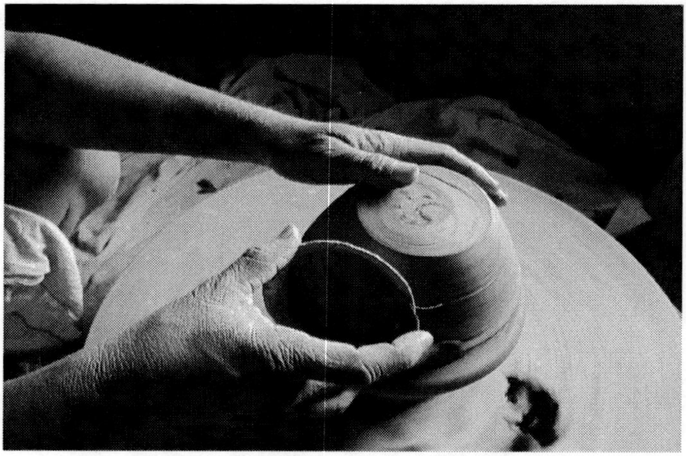

Fig. 2.16, 'scraper' scraping out the unwanted clay

Knife or 'Churiyan' (Fig. 2.17): Knife is made up of iron. This is also use for thinning the outer thick wall of the pot. This implement is noticed in Pokaran.

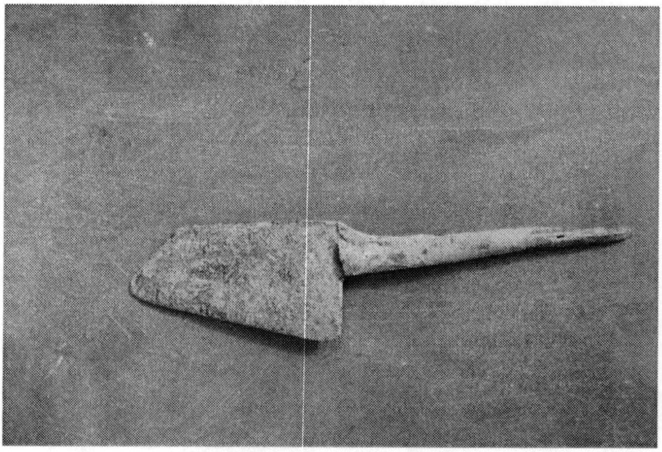

Fig. 2.17, Knife or 'Churiyan'

Thread or 'Soot': A thread is used by the potter to cut out the pot from the wheel after it is shaped (Fig. 2.18).

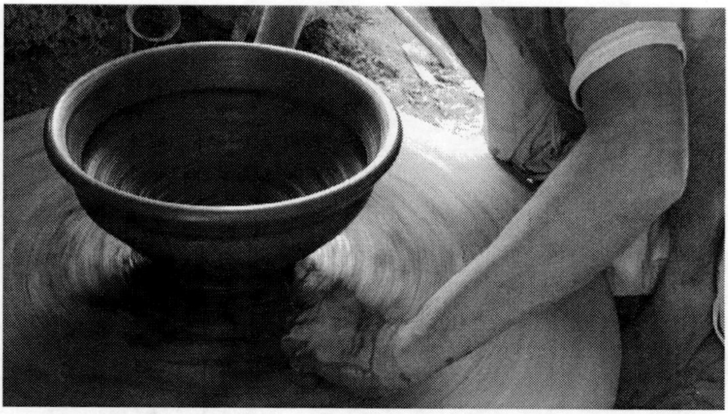

Fig. 2.18, cutting out of pot by 'Soot'

Mala (Fig. 2.19): Traditionally known as 'Mala', but it is actually a polishing tool. Its finding is from 'Molela' made up by joining each one of wild fruit seeds. When the vessels are half dried, mustard oil is applied on the surface of the pot and then it is rubbed with this 'mala' to give it a shinning surface (Fig. 2.20). In one sentence it can be said that, this tool is use for polishing earthen pots. This process is done before firing. In 'Molela' this object is known as "Kankaski mala", means a garland made up with the seeds of 'Kankas tree'.

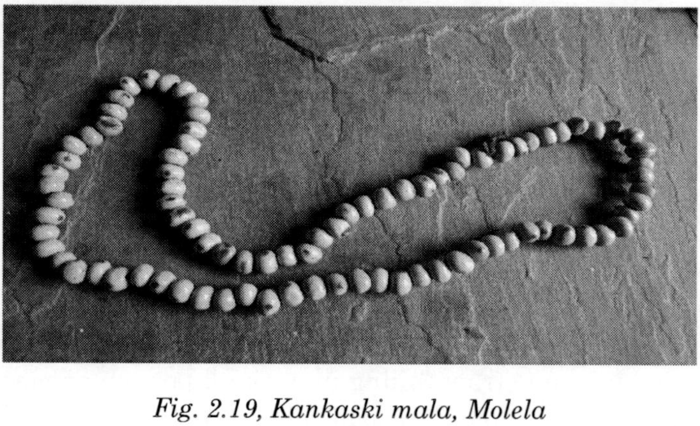

Fig. 2.19, Kankaski mala, Molela

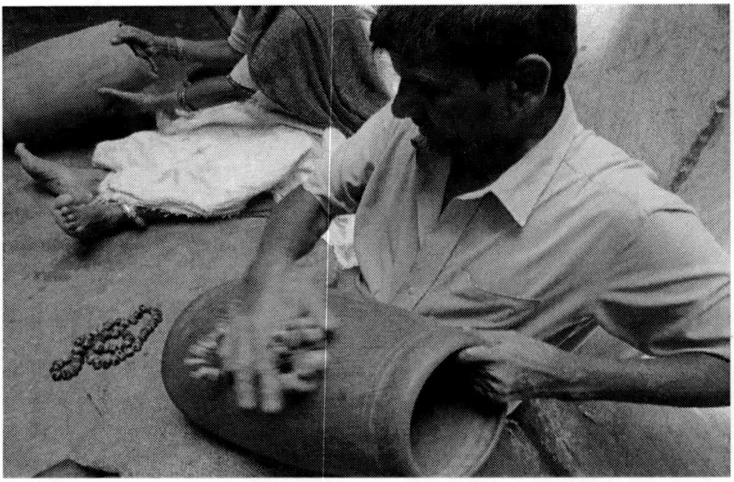

Fig. 2.20, rubbing off the surface with 'Mala'

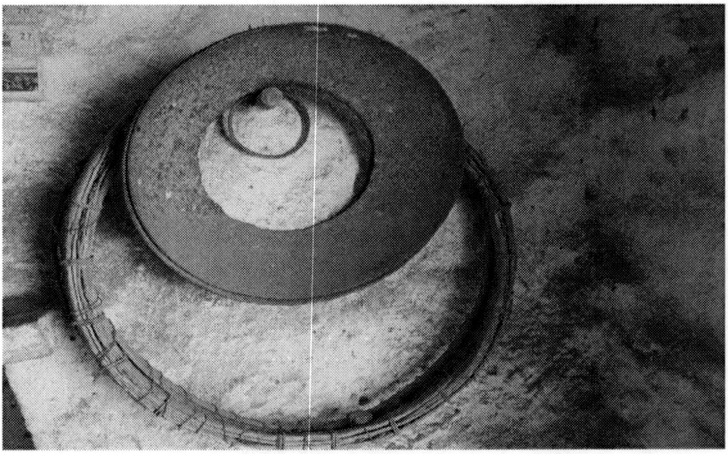

Fig. 2.21, Kuund, Pokaran

Beating base or 'Kuund' (Fig. 2.21): The traditional potter of 'Pokaran' use a base for beating the pot to give it a required form and size. In this system a supporting pad is made by using straw rolling in a round portion or mat tied in a rolled up shape. This pad raises the knees of the potter while beating. The potters of 'Pokaran' use bamboo basket and underneath it. Then it is covered up with a blanket or sack for providing a base for beating the pot. Some of the 'Kuund' are also made up of iron which provides a solid base for the vessel to set on it while beating by the potters.

DESIGNING TOOLS

Baldi (Fig. 2.22): Traditionally known as 'Baldi', it is actually a small knife or cutter. This is a region specific tool. Only the 'Molela Potters' use such kind of tools. The function of this tool is to cut out the remaining clay from the part of the terracotta block. The execution of this tool is going to be mentioned in the next chapter of 'Techniques'. Apart from cutting this is also use for designing by cutting and engraving (Fig. 2.23)

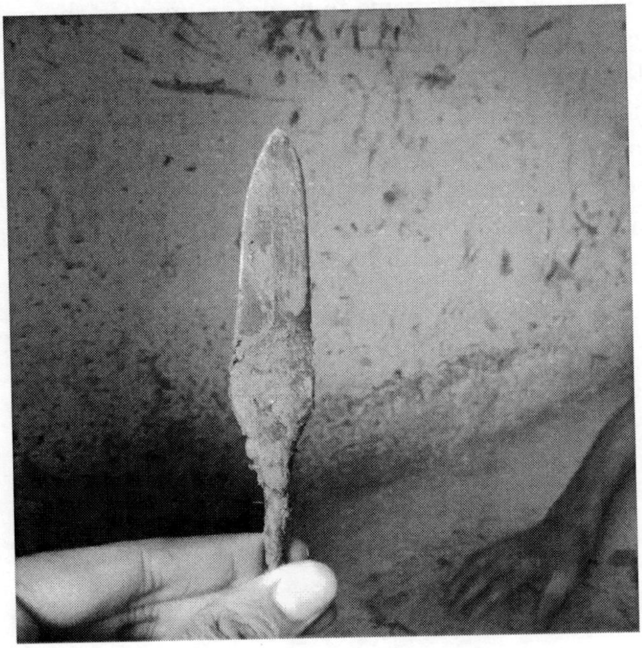

Fig. 2.22, Baldi from Molela

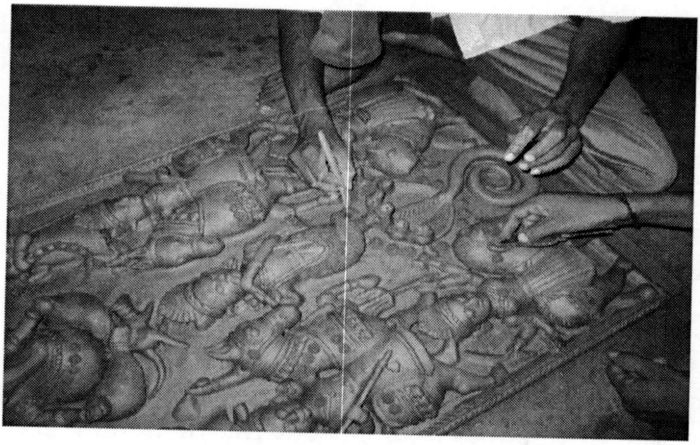

Fig. 2.23, 'Baldi' is using for designing

Singri: The name of this designing tool 'Singri' originates from a Hindi word 'singh' which means antler. Earlier, this tool was use to be made up from the antlers of Black Buck Deer. But now after the banning of deer hunting and the use of their body parts for trade by the Govt. Of India, such tools are now found made up of woods (Fig. 2.24). This is a very small tool hardly of 7 cm in length. Very few in some of the houses one can get to see the actual antler made 'Singri'. This tool is found in the house of Pokaran potters.

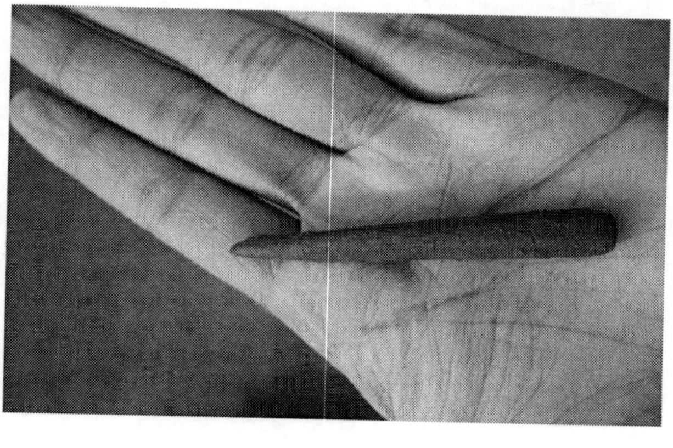

Fig. 2.24, Singri from Pokaran

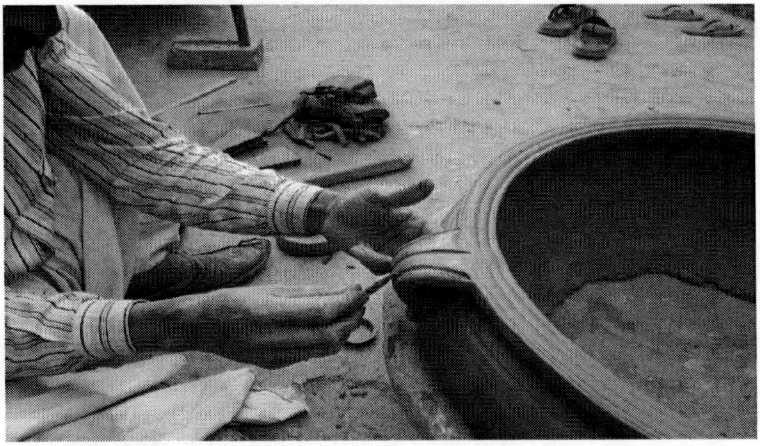

(Fig. 2.25, function of 'Singri' as a designing tool)

Khadapna: This tool is made up of wood. From this tool design is made by engraving. The size also may vary from 7 cm to 15 cm in length. The breath equally varies according to its length such as the breath of a 7 cm 'Khadapna' is 1 to 1.5 cm. Similarly a 15 cm long tool have 2 cm of breath.The naming of this tool is done on the basis of its usage. Found at both Pokaran and Molela. See Fig. 2.26, 2.27, 2.28, 2.29.

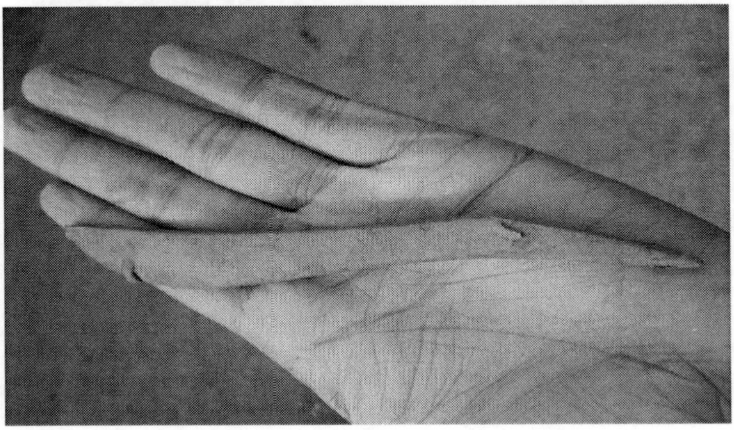

Fig.2.26, Khadapna, Pokaran

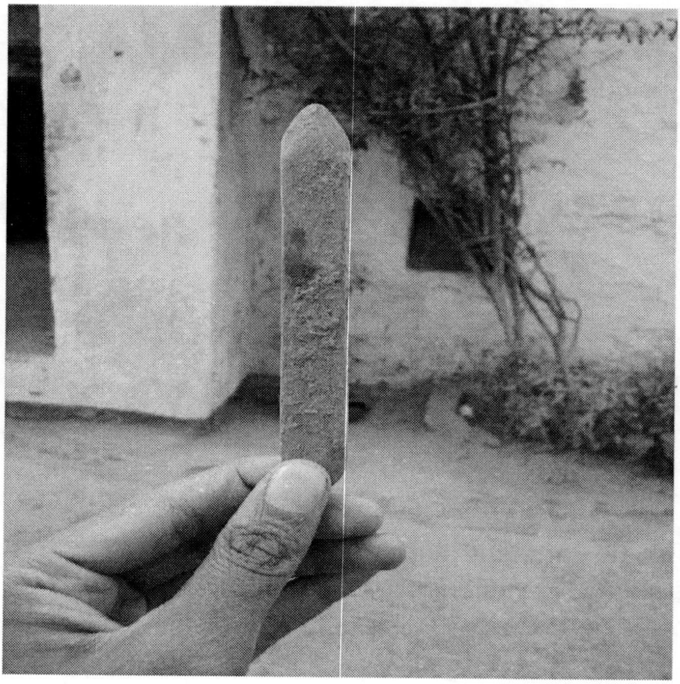

Fig. 2.27, TipoiKhadapna, Pokaran

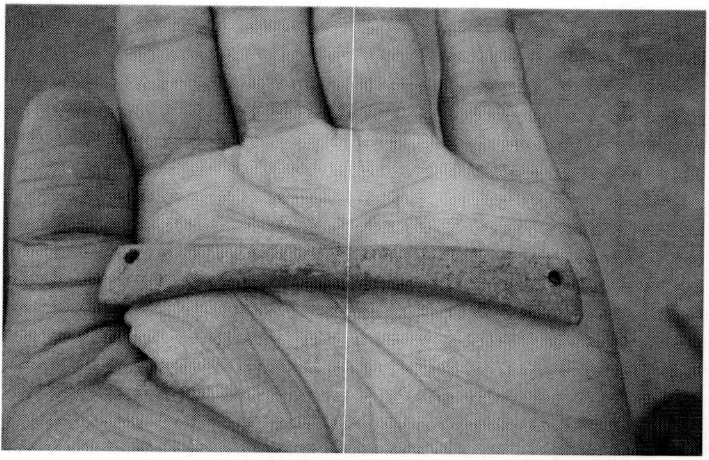

Fig. 2.28, ChotaKhadapna, Pokaran

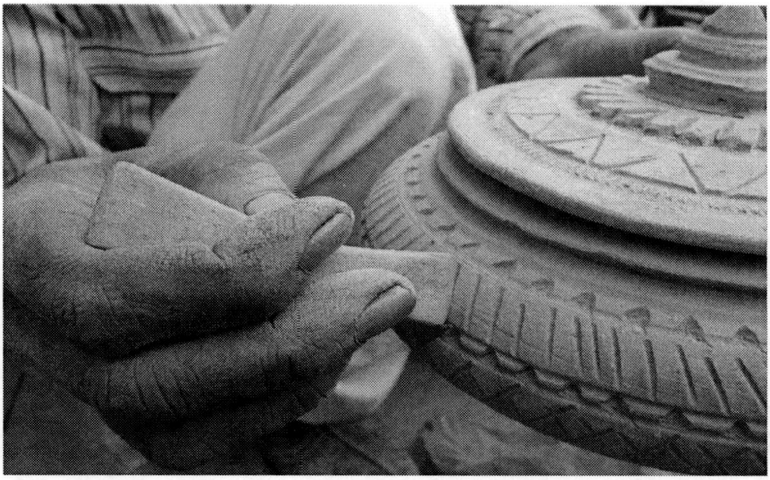

Fig. 2.29, function of Khadapna, Pokaran

Kurli: (Fig. 2.30) This tool is made up of iron or steel use as a designing tool by cutting the edges or engraved cutting(Fig. 2.31). This is an iron scraper also. Found at Pokaran.

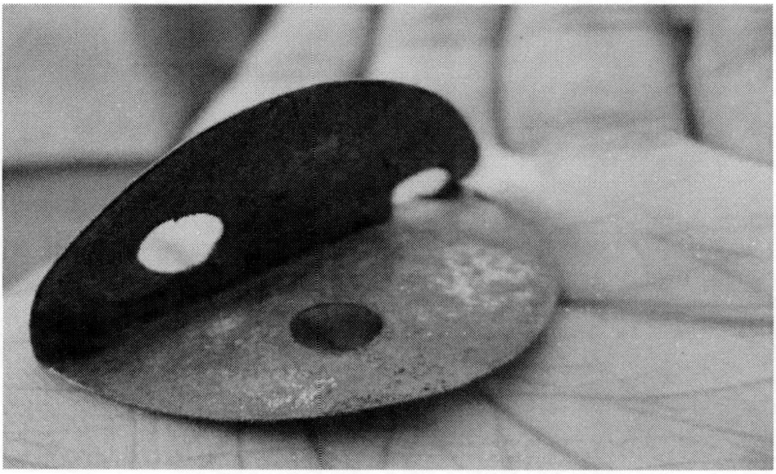

Fig. 2.30, Kurli, Pokaran

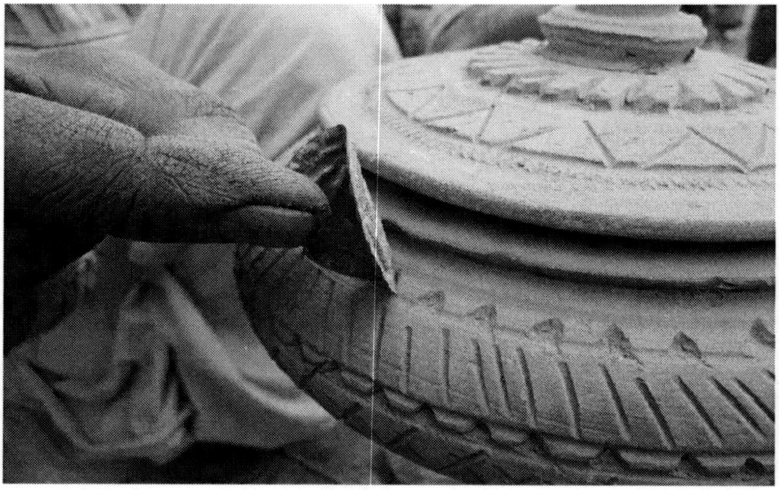

Fig. 2.31, Kurli is showing making design by engraved cutting

Leaf knife or 'Patti': (Fig. 2.32) 'Leaf knife' or 'Pen knife' or 'Patti' is a designing tool found in 'Pokaran' is made up of iron and is specially designed for perforating the pots for making it fancy and other fancy items (Fig. 2.33).

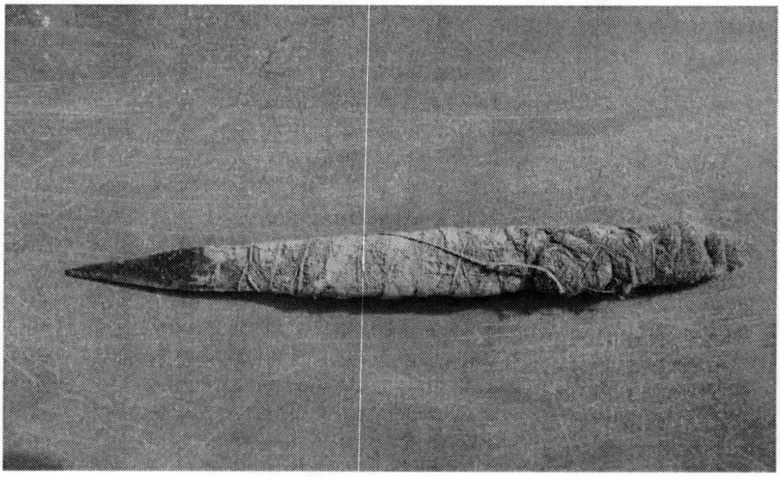

Fig. 2.32, Patti, Pokaran

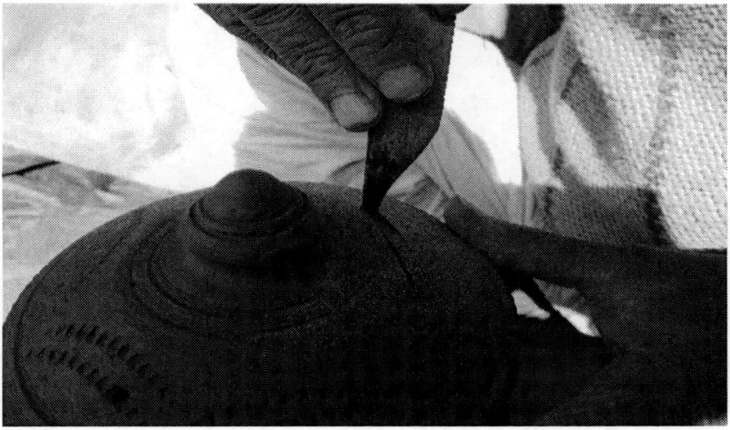

Fig. 2.33, A potter perforating the pot with a 'Patti'

Engravers: Engravers are locally called as 'Chakri' by the potters of 'Pokaran'. These are designing tools made up of iron and plastics (Fig. 2. 34). They are actually the broken parts of toys, watches and machines which are taken into uses. They are circular in shape and have teeth all around like a gear. There functions are shown in Fig. 2. 35.

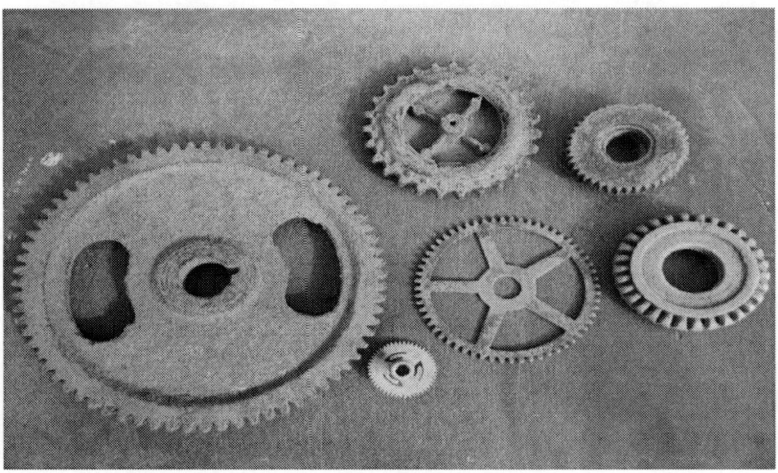

Fig. 2.34, Chakri

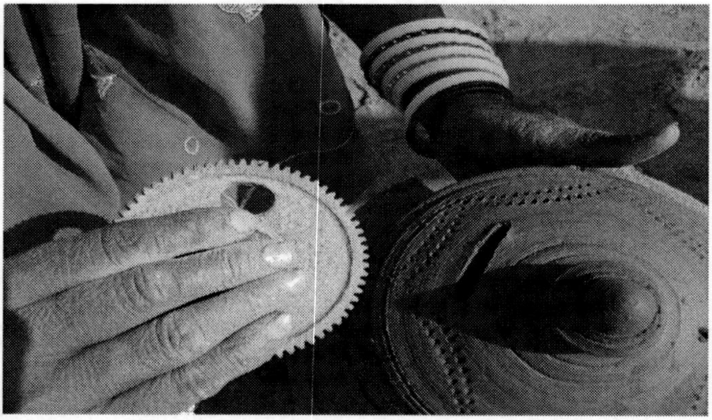

Fig. 2.35, 'Chakri' is shown how it is using for designing

Seals or 'Sancha': Various seals are used to make impression on the earthen pots and on the terracotta idols of Molela for making the jewellery designs when they are partly dried. Seals are made up of baked clay or wood made by the potters themselves. The seals contains geometric designs, faces of deities, floral and faunal impression etc. Locally also termed as 'Thappa'. The following figures show some of them.

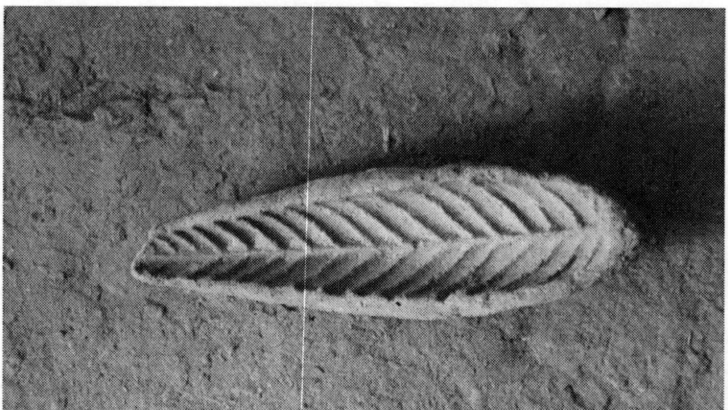

Fig. 2.36,

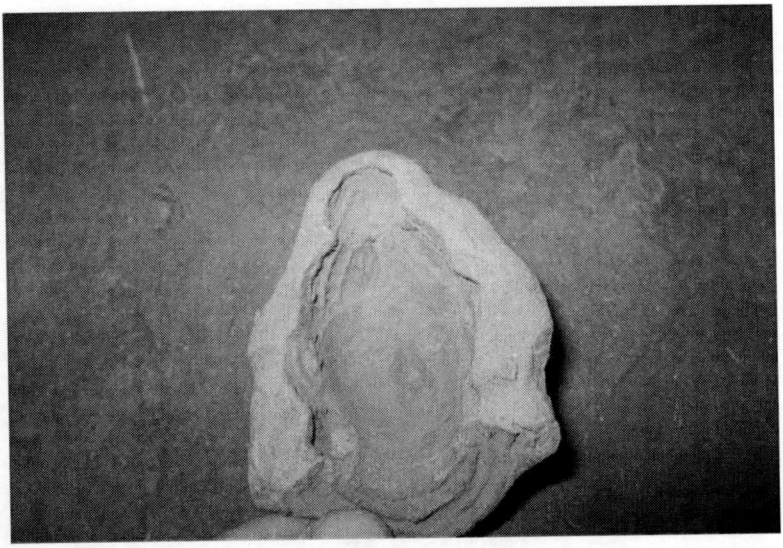

Fig. 2.37,

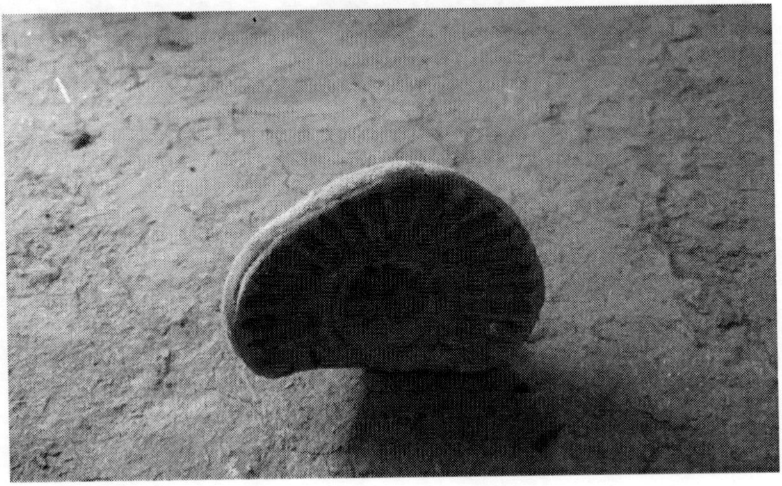

Fig. 2.38,

Brushes: Brushes are the painting tools use only in case of painted pottery and for the painting of votive terracotta idols. Those brushes are easily available in the local market, but one distinct thing I have noticed in Pokaran. The potters of Pokaran use a special kind of brush which is made from the hairs of donkeys. The hairs are cut from the upper portion of the donkey's neck. Then the bunch of hairs are cut all together into its requiredshape and tied up with a thread. Another feature is that those brushes don't have any sick or holder like the other paint brush. (Fig. 2.39)

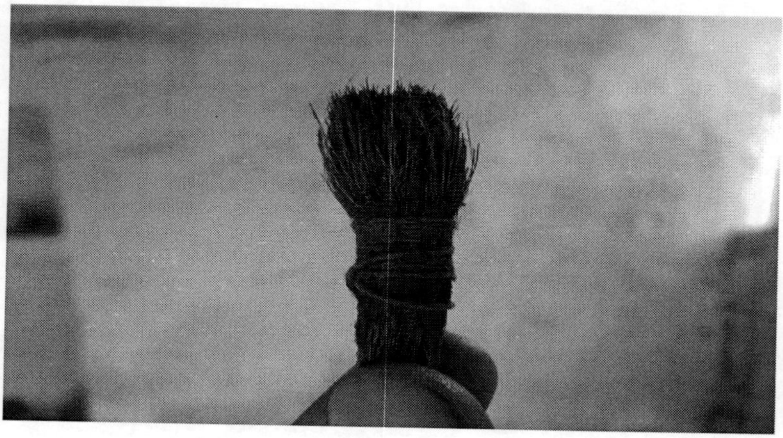

Fig. 2.39, brush made up with donkey's hair, Pokaran

4

TECHNIQUES

If we look into the soil types of India, we can get to see the wide varieties of clay spreading in different parts of India have difference in composition, texture and colour. All types of clay are not suitable for making all types of pottery. Raw materials which are required for making pottery and terracotta are clay, temper and water. These materials are easily available in their natural environment and do not require much monitory investment. It can also be said as a free gift of nature.

Longevity and good finishing of pottery depend upon the quality of clay. Hence, the selection of clay suitable for pottery is very much essential. This knowledge can be gained with the help of experienced or old potter who can recognise the clay by seeing its colour and texture. A real potter is who, who can easily recognise the quality of clay by first sight.

Clay can be dug from river bed, pond side or from fallow land. The potters of 'Molela' bring their clay from a pond which is situated on the bank of 'River Banas,'which is hardly 2- 3 km away from 'Molela' (Fig.3.1). Another site is situated in the other hand corner of the village which is also about 2 km away. 'Molela' clay is muddy is colour and best suits for making terracotta plaques and idols. The potters of 'Pokaran' bring their soil from 'Rann', a fallow land which is the salt range of Pokaran (Fig. 3.2). This salt range is situated at a distance of about 8 km away from Pokaran. At the 'Rann' there are three types of soil are found viz. soil with gravel mixture, salty soil and the fine one. The fine one is suitable for pottery. One thing is also to be mentioned that the soil of 'Pokaran' contain high range of 'silica' which makes the pottery hard and durable after baking. That's why 'Pokaran' soil is best suits for making pottery.

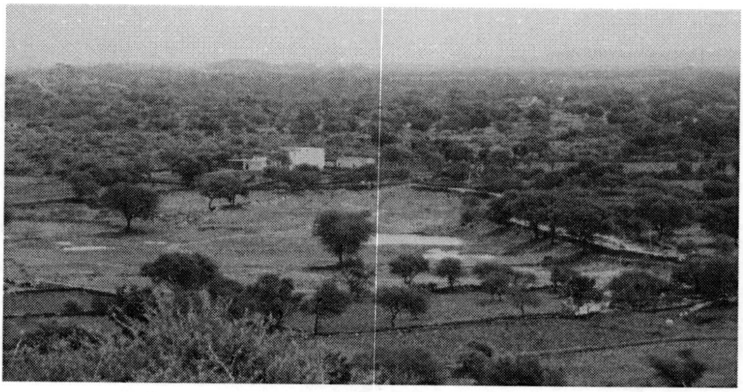

Fig. 3.1, site from where the Molela potters bring their soil

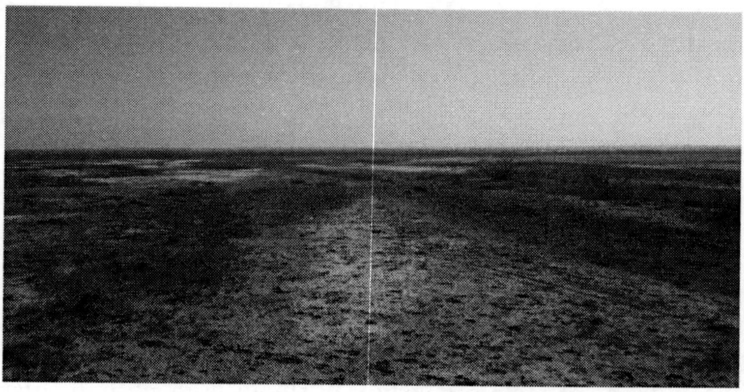

Fig. 3.2, Rann, Pokaran

The upper part of the land surface generally do not use for making pottery because it contain lots of impurities. The first work of the potter is to survey the entire area and whenever suitable clay deposit is found they start digging. Before starting the digging, they first test the upper surface by digging it a bit upto 2 meter vertically (Fig. 3.3).

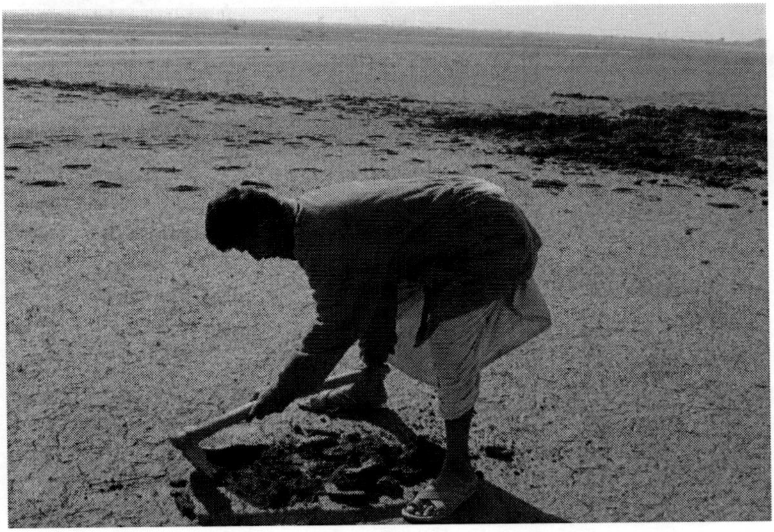

Fig. 3.3, potter testing the soil before final digging

Then if they found the area is suitable for digging they continue to excavate vertically for 3- 4 metres without disturbing the remaining areas. The knowledge of testing the soil and finding out the exact soil suitable for their product is gained by their long time experience.

In the procedure of their digging method they first dig out the soil with the help of spade of shovel. Then they kneade the soil with both hands by splashing water at regular interval. This process is continued for minimum 5 minutes. In this process the primary impurities like gravel, roots of plants, sand particles, etc. were removed (Fig. 3.4)

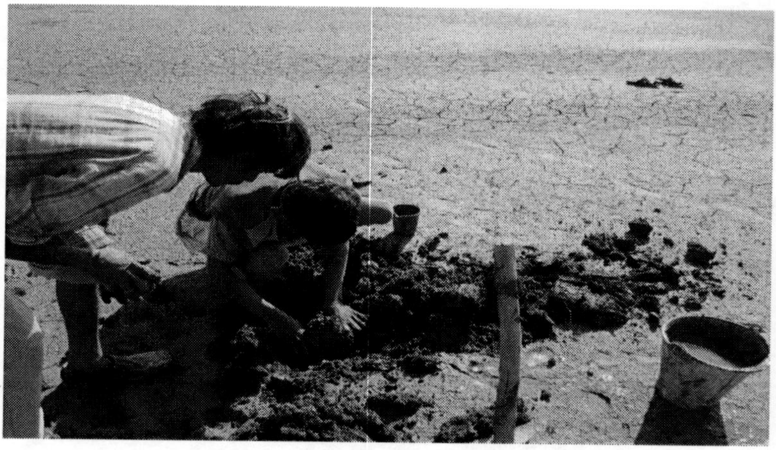

Fig. 3.4, potter showing kneading the soil

After the kneading procedure is completed, they make clay balls with that kneaded soil and go on making these and dumped it on a big polythin sheet which is later wrapped with that polythin sheet to prevent the penetration of air. This entire cycle is continued for the entire day until and unless they meet their required soil demand. The following figures, (Fig. 3.5, 3.6, 3.7) furnished the entire sequence.

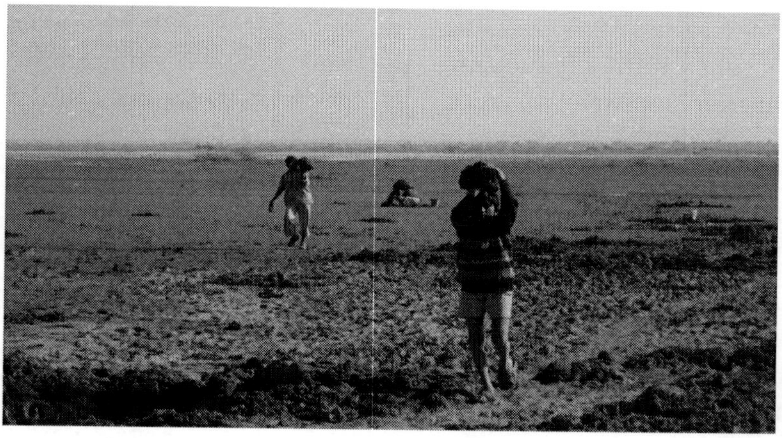

Fig. 3.5, a boy carrying the clay ball

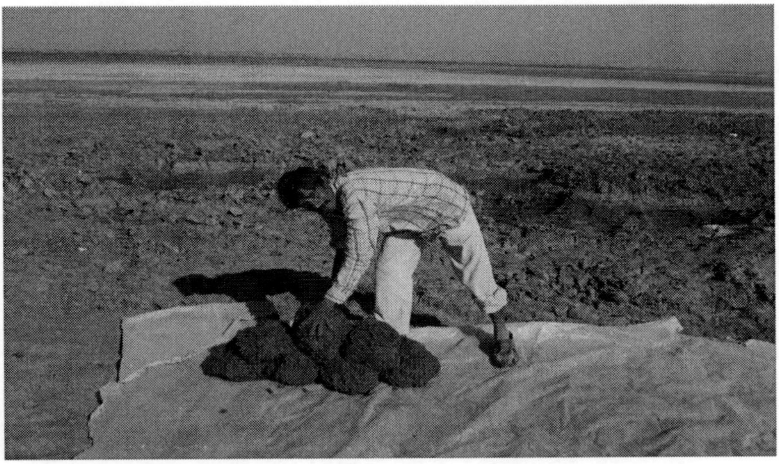

Fig. 3.6, a man depositing clay balls on a big polythin sheet

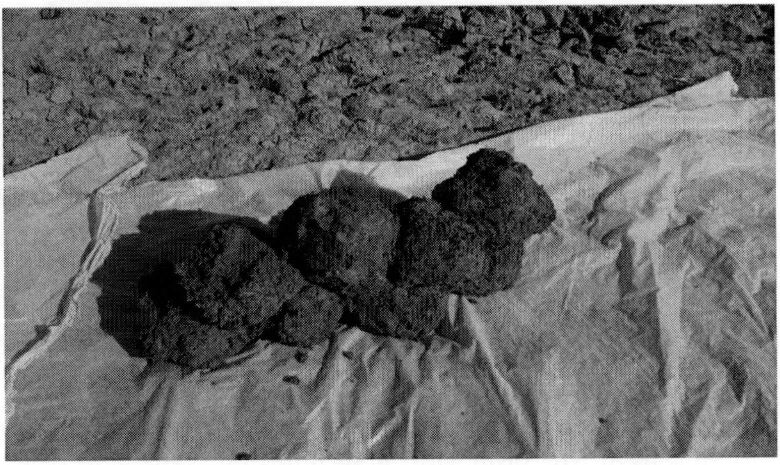

Fig. 3.7, dumped clay balls

The digged out clay then brought in home by means of bullock cart or trailor attached to a tractor or even on small truck. These means of transport is specially employed for bringing large quantity of soil. The soil is generally collected and stacked during summer in large quantity because the sites are then dried. During the time of monsoon the rain water bring the alluvial soil with all its impurities and make their deposits. Soon after the monsoon the entire region is water logged and allow the soil to rot which is very essential to make the soil suitable for pottery making.

The collected soil is stored either in a large open varandah or in the store room. Generally the potters of Rajasthan do not prefer to store the clay in shade. They believe that the quality of clay get improved if it is exposed to sun, wind and water.

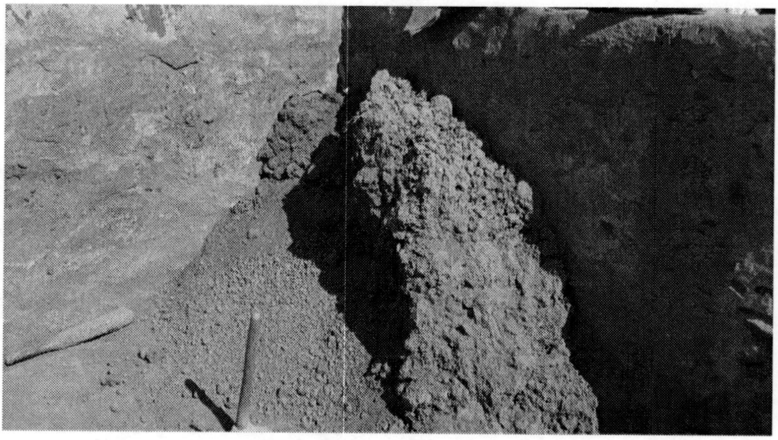

Fig. 3.8, soil stored in an open pavilion

Next comes the task of preparation of soil. "An old potter from Rajasthan said that the greatest skill of the potter lies in his ability of preparing clay suitably. The methods of preparation differ largely from region to region according to the nature of the locally available clays. But there are certainstandardized processes which are adopted by potters all over the country." (Saraswati and Behura, 1966). The following are the methods of preparation of soil. Saraswati and Behura has mentioned three steps by using the term 'cleaning', 'kneading' and 'mixing'.

At first the clay is exposed under the sun and then spread out in an open area. Larger impurities are removed by hands. Then the clay clods are rammedwith a wooden club locally known as 'Mokhdi'. By ramming the clay clods are pulverized. In the third stage of filtering of clay, the clays are filtered with 'challni'. In this method, most of the impurities are removed.

In the next step after the clay is pulverized and dried, the potters put it into water which is stored either into a pit or in a large urn (Fig. 3.9).

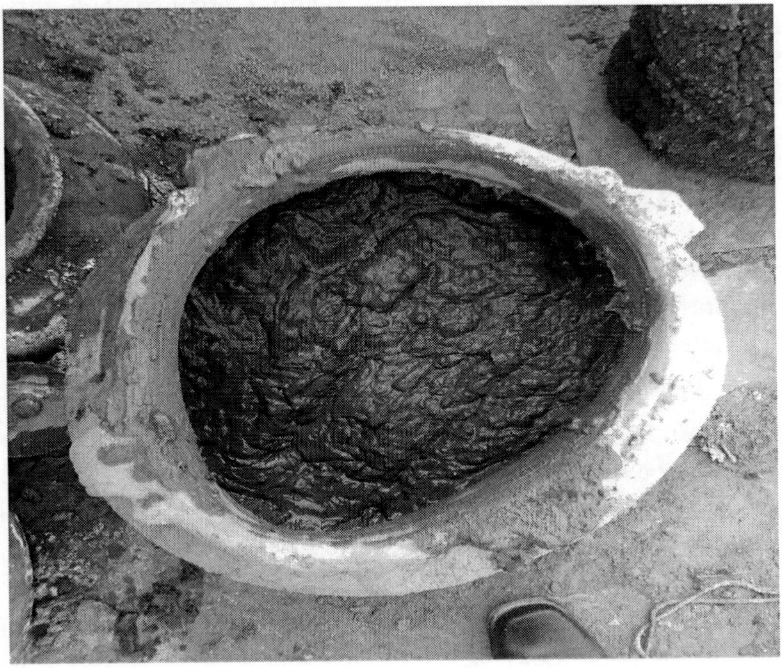

Fig. 3.9, clay is moist with water in an urn

In this way the clay is moisten in water for one day. In the following day the saturated clay is bring out from the pit or urn and again filtered with 'challni'. In the above mentioned method the entire impurities were removed and the soil turned out to a fine one.

In the third stage of mixing, there comes the crucial part of preparation of clay. An appropriate mixing of temper and other type of clay requires high level of knowledge which is related with the chemical reaction of some clay. So, when needed more than one variety of clay and temper is mixed to meet the required proportion to make their product. In many times the potter does not find that satisfied quality of clay suited for pottery. So, in order to improving clay quality tempering and mixing of other clay is necessary. Tempering materials such as husk, dung, saw dust, etc. are used. If the temper is not mixed properly then it looses its pliability and the pot will crack.

In the following stanzas, I am mentioning about the techniques which the potters apply for making their terracotta objects and pottery. Further I am mentioning that the potter of 'Molela' is famous for their rich terracotta art which depicts terracotta plaques and figurines and the 'Pokaran' potters are well known for their pottery. So, here I am starting with the methods of 'Molela' potters.

For making their terracotta plaques 'Molela' potters use two types of soils. The finer one locally known as 'Awla' and the soil contain sand particles known as 'Nada'. Both of these soils are mixed together. For tempering donkey dung powder is also added in the ratio of 1:3. Briefly describing they mix 40 % fine soil, 40 % sandy soil and 20 % of donkey dung powder to make the entire mixture suitable for making their plaques. First of all the soils are all saturated with water for the night. After bringing the donkey dung they are kept under the sun for completely drying it up. Once it dried up the dung is rammed until and unless it becomes powder. The other waste materials and unwanted substances are removed. Later the dung powder is shifted to their store room (Fig. 3.10).

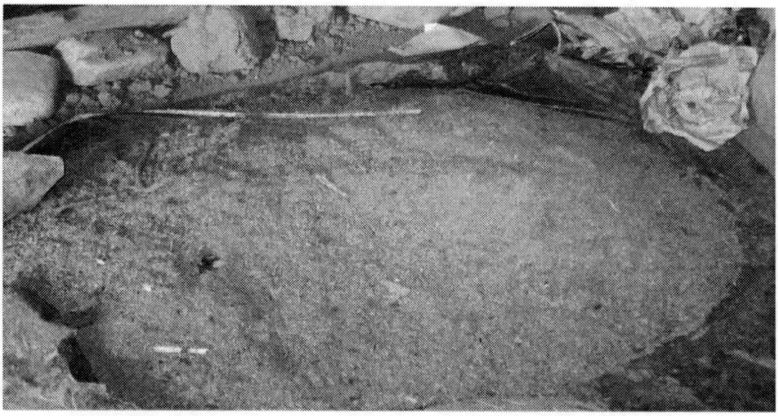

Fig. 3.10, donkey dung

The mixing of clay is done by foot. The clay and the temper material are spread over the yard and then water is added with bucket. The potter smashes the mixture with foot by circling manner on the clay mixture as shown in fig. 3. 11.

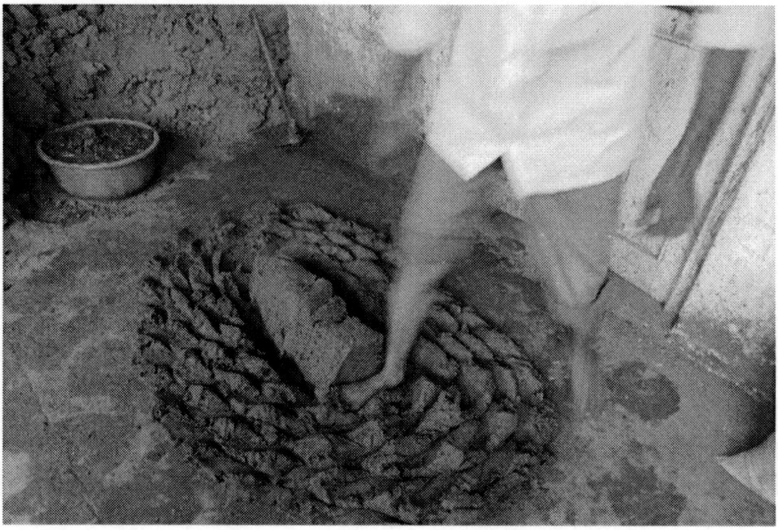

Fig. 3.11, potter smashing the clay

This procedure is continued for repeated times until and unless it mixed properly and shown no lumps. Then they cut out the clay balls out of that mixture and wrap it in plastic to avoid contact with air.

After the preparation, the first step comes for giving shape to that clay ball. Firstly, donkey dung powder is spread over the ground so that the clay does not stick to the ground. Then required amount of clay is separated from the clay stock and flattened over the ground with 'patiya'. Further, water is added for flattening and smoothening the plaque (Fig. 3.12). After the clay get flattened and received its required thickness a frame is placed on the slab to give it a require shape. The thickness of the slab varies according to its size. The frame is used to give a required shape to the slab. The slab is made with oval shape top or square or rectangular. After placing the frame, the required shape is created and the extra part were detached from the main slab with a tool named 'baldi' (Fig. 3. 13).

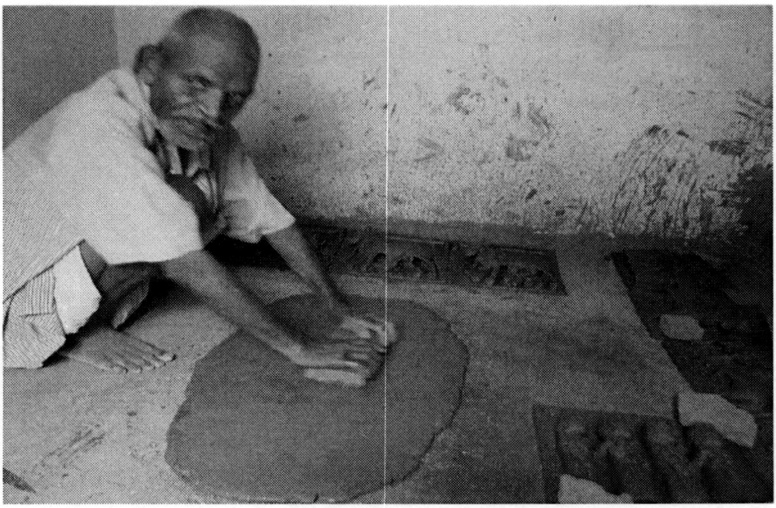

Fig. 3.12, potter smoothening the slab with 'patiya'

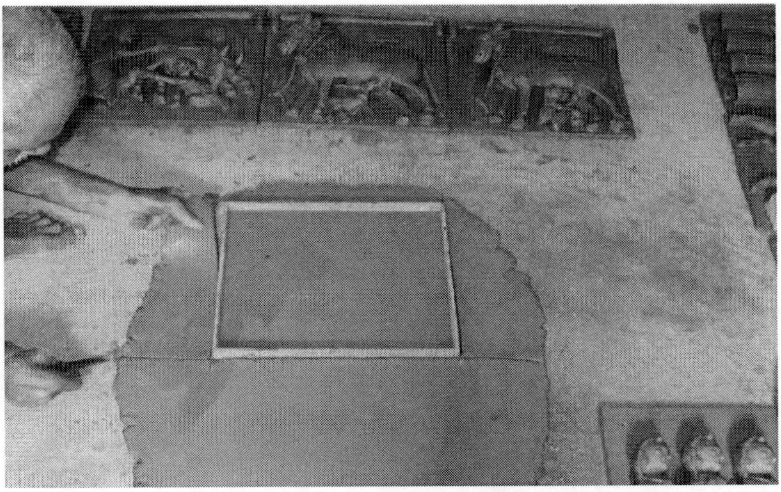

Fig. 3.13, excess part is cutting off

In this manner the slabs are created and further smoothen with 'pindi'. The separated slabs are kept aside (Fig. 3.14).

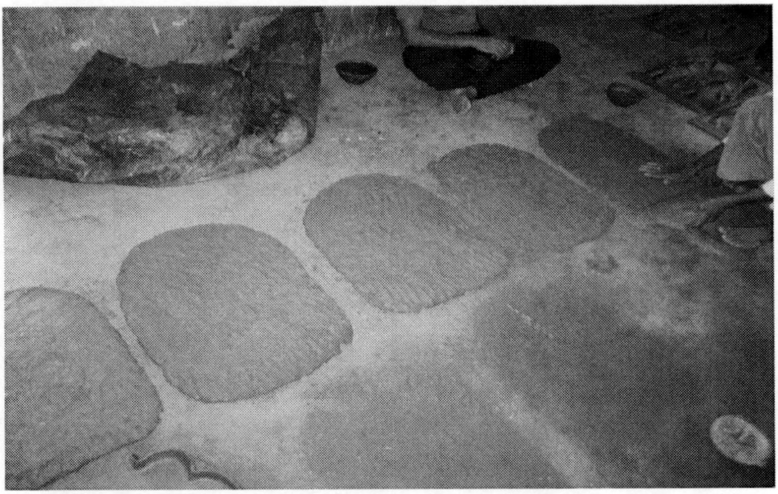

After this appropriate measurement are taken with palm and cluster of fingers and the surface is smoothen by hand (Fig. 3.15). The clay which are separated from the main slabs are used for making the figures which are going to be added to that slab. In this way the flattened clay pieces and coils are added to the main slab to give it a shape (Fig. 3.16). The edges of the slab are also raised like a wall to form the rim of the slab.

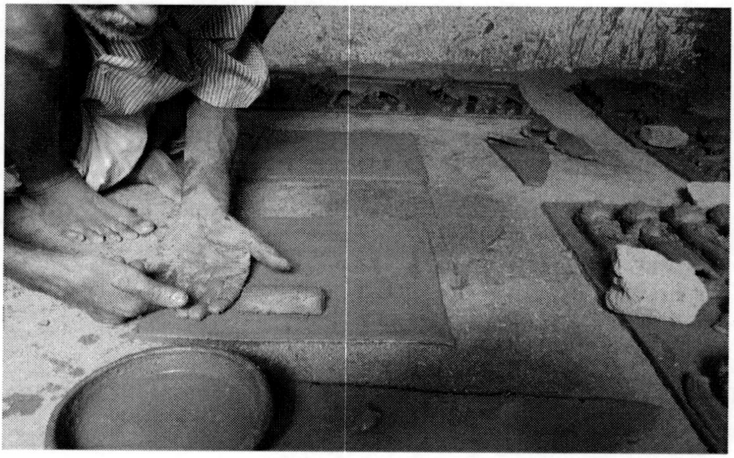

Fig. 3.15, a potter taking finger measurement for his plaque

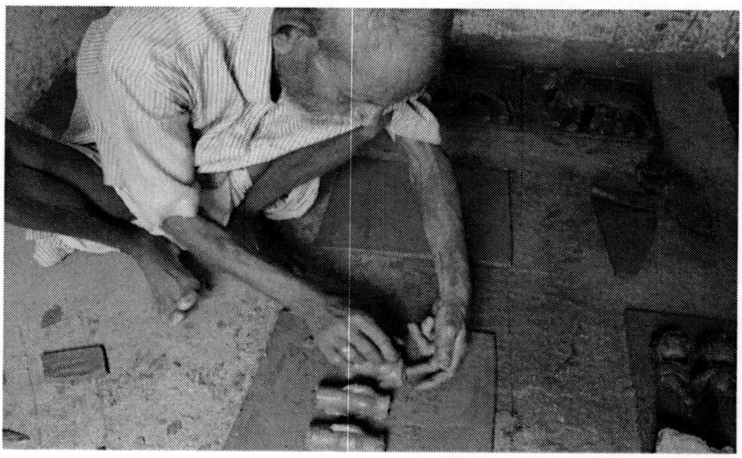

Fig. 3.16, figurines are added on the slab

The figurines are thus formed with fingers as shown in fig. 3.16. Slowly slowly all the other parts of the body are also added by hand. One of the interesting feature is that Molela potters simply use hand forming technique and they make their each items by hand. The figures which are added to the slab are made hollow from inside (Fig. 3.17) so that they do not crack or burst while baking inside the kiln. Another reason is that it also reduces the weight of that plaque. Plaques made with solid figurines also consume more fuel for baking which is also highly non- economic.

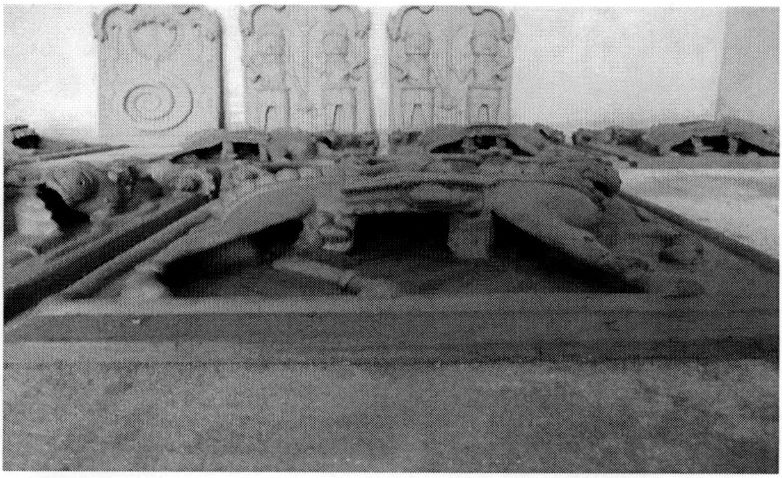

Fig. 3. 17, figure added to the slab are made hollow

Further detailing were done by adding accessories like jewellery, weapons and other props on them. Jewellery were made with tiny clay balls. Thin coils are also made for this purpose. Terracotta seals and casts are also use for engraving different designs. Apart from it various designing tools are also used for making various patterns and designs on their terracotta plaques.

Another matter is noticed that, all the terracotta and pottery making works are done on the kaccha floor which is made up of the mixture of cow dung and mud generally seen in all Indian villages. As water is needed for making any earthen object.After forming those kaccha articles was left in their workshop for drying up in room temperature. While working with mud and clay, the kacchafloor use to soak the excess water from the earthen materials and facilitate the process of drying up. Before exposing under the sunlight the terracotta articles are kept inside the shade for five to seven days. They generally avoid concrete floor. The final drying up process took up for next two to three days under the clear sky before putting inside the kiln.

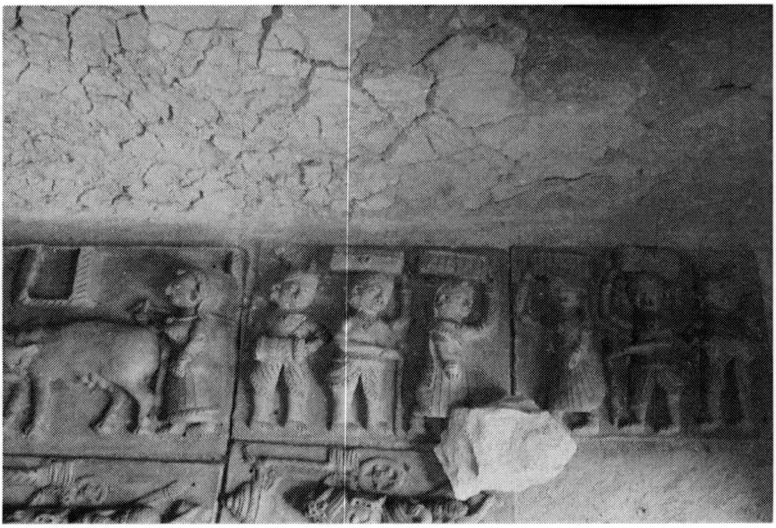

Fig. 3.18, finished plaques are kept for drying in shed

The art of making pottery can be conducted by both throwing at wheel and handmade. Throwing of a heap of clay on wheel and giving it an artistic shape is a fascinating job. The potters of Pokaran are expertise in this field. Pottery tradition of Pokaran are very old and are of wheel made. As I have already observed the wheel made pottery at Pokaran, so in this report I am going to describe only about the wheel made pottery. The potters learn this art from their childhood and gradually became master in this field by practise. In this method the potters of Pokaran adopted the same method of preparation of soil which the Molela potters possess. But there is a bit difference. The potters of Pokaran never mix any other clay within it neither they use any temperament. They make out their pot out of only one type of clay. This is the speciality of the 'Pokaran' clay which does not require any further treatment. After moistening the clay by keeping it in water, they take the clay out and knead it with the mixing of dry soil (Fig. 3.19).

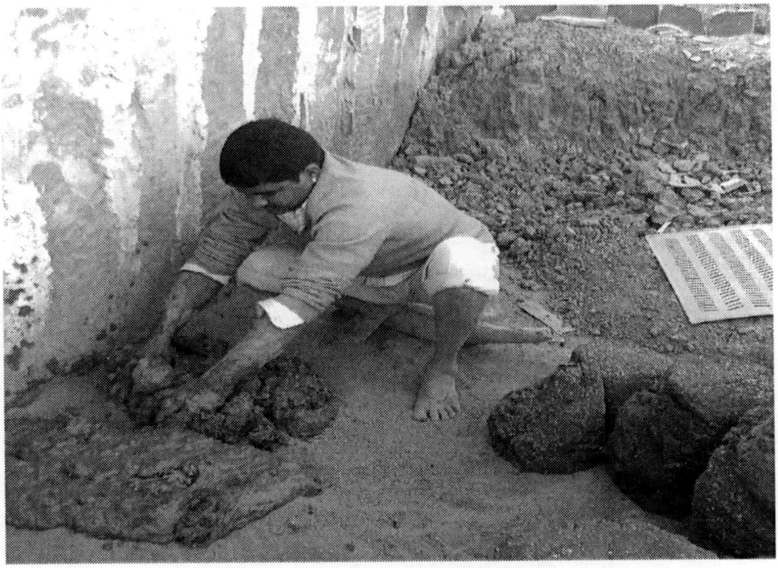

Fig. 3.19, kneading of clay

Before starting the process of wheel throwing, the potter separate the required amount of prepared clay from the heap and knead it once again as show in fig. 3.20. After the final kneading a heap of clay is prepared either in the form of a cylinder of ball. The size may vary according to the type of pot they want to make.

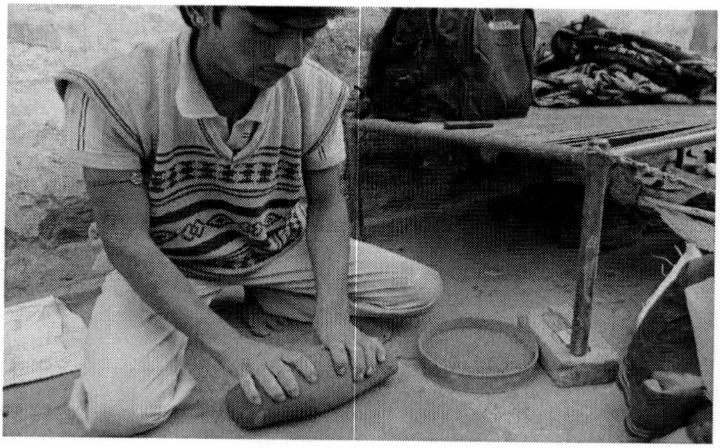

Fig. 3.20, final kneading before throwing

The potter generally takes out separate clay lump for each pots but sometimes more than one pot can also be prepared from a single lump of clay. In the wheel throwing method a lump of clay is placed in the centre of the wheel. The potter rotates the wheel with the stick in a clock wise direction and when the wheel receives its maximum speed, the clay is thrown on it (Fig. 3.21).

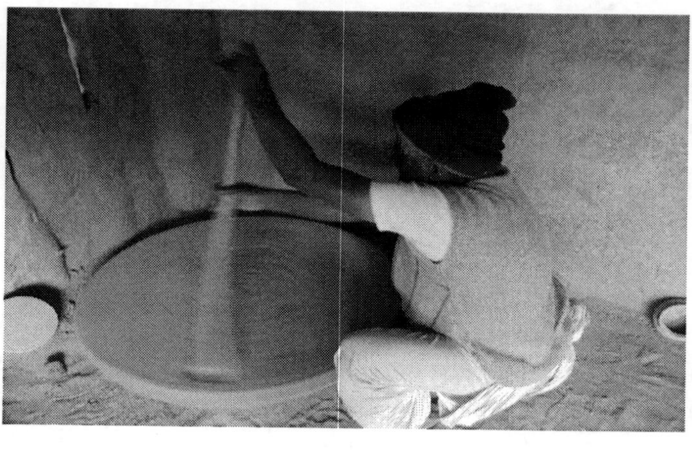

Fig. 3.21, potter rotating wheel

After throwing, the potter have to undergo various stages before giving the lump of clay into a desired shape. He use to function his fingers by manipulating it in many ways. Those functions are as follows:

When the wheel rotating fast, the clay lump is gently pressed with both the palms and the fingers are joined at the other side. In this way by balancing the function of both palms and fingers the clay lump is slowly rises up (Fig. 3.22)

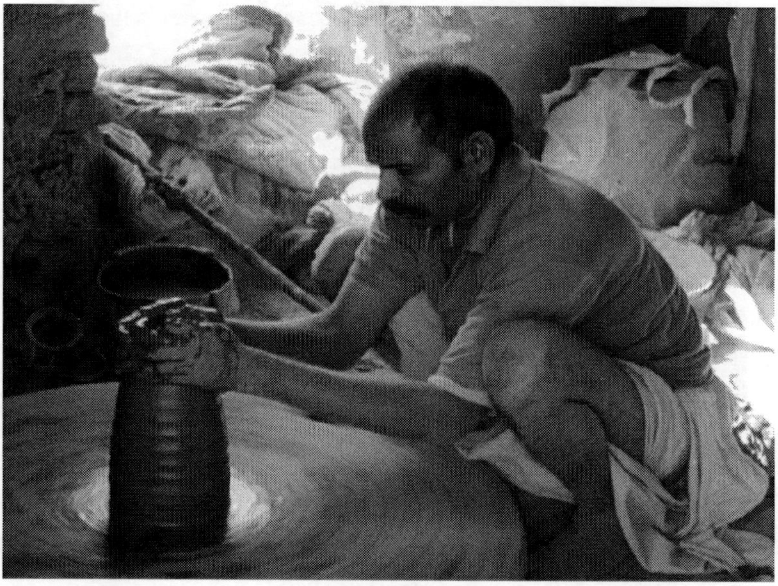

Fig. 3.22,

In the next step, the dome structure which is formed is pressed again in downward by keeping the fingers of both the hand vertically on the upper rim. Then the fingers are all bend. Slowly slowly the finger get separated and make an opening in the dome (Fig.3.23)

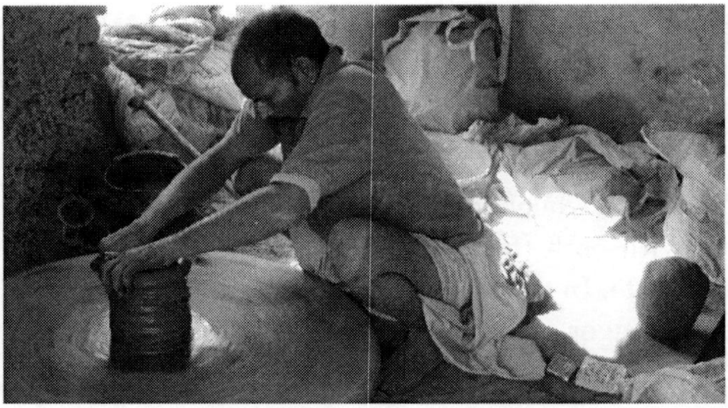

Fig. 3.23,

After pressing down and creating an opening, the cylindrical shape reduces once again to its original size. In this stage, the clay is again drawn up by creating a gently pressure on the clay wall from bottom to top. When the rising clay reaches its upper limit both the thumbs meet (Fig 3.24).

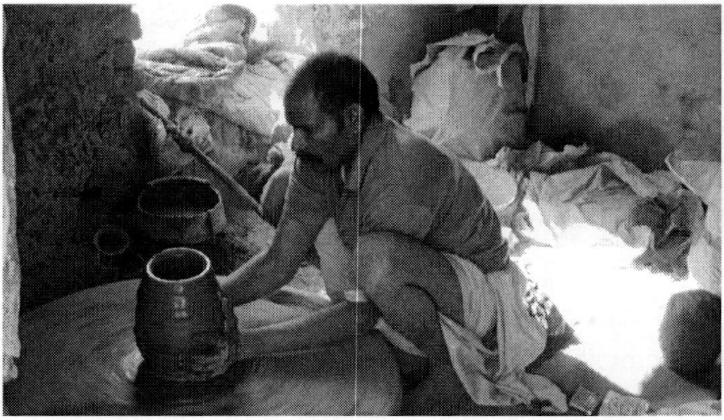

Fig. 3.24,

For making the collar of a pot the four fingers of the left hand inside the neck of the cylinder and the thumb outside, the potter joins his right hand thumb finger close to the left and gently gives pressure to the neck. The same procedure is repeated by changing the position of fingers (Fig. 3.25).

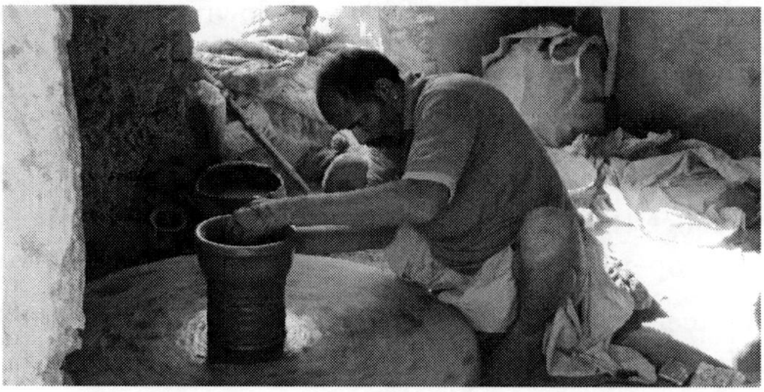

Fig. 3.25,

The collaring stage is then followed by thinning. The wall which has been created by drawing up and down is thick. It requires thinning. In this method the potter put his left hand inside the clay cylinder and the outer wall is supported by his right hand so that the cylinder does not get deshaped. The inner wall is pressed by the left hand and simultaneously the outer wall is pressed and supported by the right palm. Both the hands moved in a balanced way so that the cylinder gets an even thickness. In this process almost the final shape is prepared (Fig. 3.26).

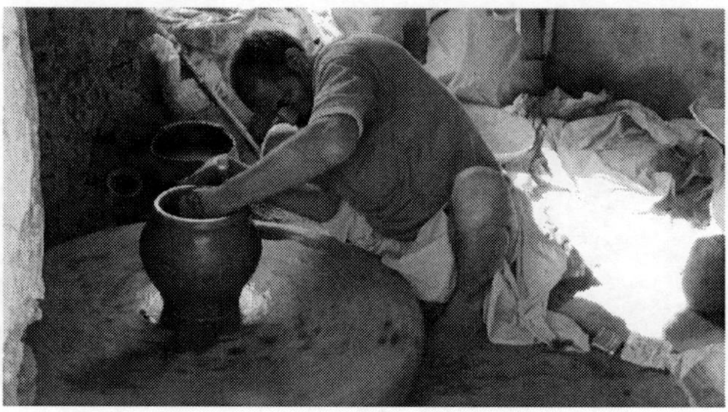

Fig. 3.26,

At last stage the finished pot is cutted off by a thread and removed from the wheel. In this entire process, I noticed that two times the wheel get slowed down and the potter again speeded up the wheel. The time taken in finishing all the stages of throwing is five minutes. There are some factors such as the size of the clay lump, the strength of the potter for revolving the wheel, dimension of the wheel, etc. also influence the time taken working on wheel. The whole function is operated carefully by an experienced hand.

The technique of enlarging by patting is applicable mainly for hand made pottery but some wheel made pottery at Pokaran also requires this further treatment. Except for some of the earthen wares such as cups, plates, toys, etc. all other wares require this treatment. After removing the pot from the wheel thick layer of clay remains at the bottom. The pots are not directly exposed to sunlight after removal from the wheel because excess heat can make it hard and also may crack down the product. The 'kaccha' pots are first of all dried by keeping it in sand for overnight. The sand absorbs the moisture of the pot. There should be a perfect balance i.e. neither the pot should be too hard nor should be wet.

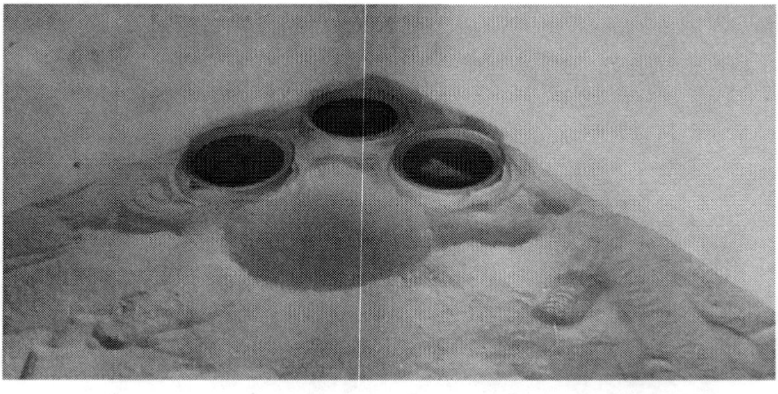

Fig. 3.27, pots kept inside the sand for drying

When the pot is half dried, it is taken out in the following morning for patting. In this method, the potter holds the stone 'pindi' i.e. the anvil in his left hand and put his hand inside the pot and started patting it with 'thapa' with his right hand. Anvil is used to give support to the wall while patting. In this stage, the pot is placed on the beating base and the bottom of the pot facing towards the right hand side of the potter. At first, the bottom of the pot is enlarged. In the second stage of patting, the shoulder part of the pot is patted with the same anvil and beater. And at last, the potter takes an anvil having convex working side and the pot is patted from top to bottom very carefully by turning the pot in its beating base. At last the pot gets enlarged and gets its required thinness and size. The entire process took about ten to fifteen minutes for each pot. In a single day, a potter can finish twenty five pots. In 'Pokaran' sand is largely used for this purpose. Sand prevent the anvil and the beater for sticking to the pot. The beater and the anvil also saturated with water at regular intervals. A potter always keep by his side a container with water and a piece of cloth or sponge. Another thing is to be noted that when enlargement is not required in case of small pottery, the thick clay layer at the bottom is removed by using a scraper by slowly turning the in anti- clock wise direction.

FIRING TECHNIQUE

Baking of pottery is a very laborious job. It includes a series of problems. A potter should be highly experienced, otherwise their entire effort would be dismantled. It needed a very careful observation. If heat is not given properly then the pot will remain kaccha and excessive heat will also crack down the pottery. The potters of India practised practised the technique of firing. This method can be broadly divided into two types namely, firing in a kiln and open firing. The potters of Molela uses the kiln method. In local term, the kiln is known as 'bhatti'. Generally the 'bhatti' is situated at the back yard of their house or inside the courtyard. On the day of firing the clay articles such as pots, terracotta plaques, toys, etc. are brought to the spot by the potter accompanied by his wife and children. The articles are once again exposed under the sun for the final drying. The firing starts usually in the evening. The potter of Molela construct their kiln in raised form which looks like a well from outside. It is very simple in construction and can retain heat for a longer time. The kiln is constructed with bricks, mud and also the bricks are joined with cement. The size of the kiln vary but most of the kiln are of 4 ft to 5 ft in height and 5 ft in diameter (Fig. 3. 28). At the bottom, a bit raised from the ground iron net platform is placed known as 'loohekamachan'.

In this method, before firing, first of all 'Ganapati', is placed on the iron platform. Its their symbolic ritual. Then the terracotta plaques are piled in the circular manner across the wall of the kiln. The bigger plaques are placed at the bottom and gradually the smaller plaques are placed at the top in ascending order. In between two plaques a gap is maintained which is made by placing pot sherds in between them. At a time in a single kiln fifty to sixty plaques along with other articles can be baked. After that the entire pile is covered with broken pieces of pots from the top. It is done to retain the heat inside the kiln. Fire is lightened from the fire hole situated at the bottom of the kiln. The fire intensity is low at the initial stage and gradually it increases. The area under the iron raised platform is filled up with dung cakes, woods and husks so that fire can be ignited quickly. Gradually the intensity of heat is raised by pushing woods from the firing channel. After the 'bhatti' get totally heated upto 700°C - 800°C the pot sherds covering the top is removed so that excess heat and smoke can be released.

After this maximum temperature reached, the potter stop putting further fuel into it.The kiln is then left for two to three days for cooling.

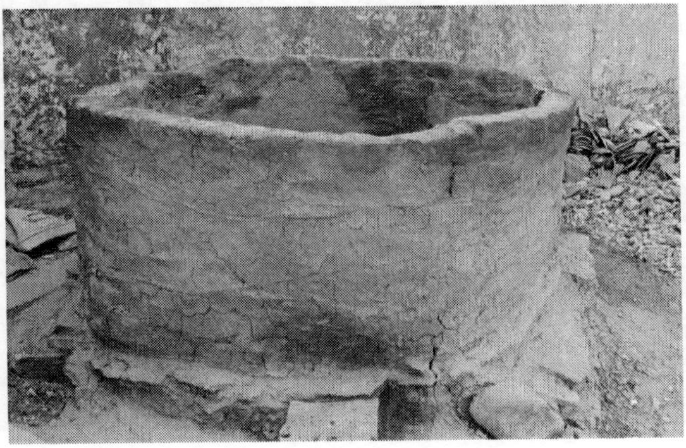

Fig. 3. 28, kiln

On the other hand the potters of Pokaran practise open firing system. In this method capital investment is very much needed for the raw materials. Now a days it became quite costly. Raw materials needed for firing are wood (Fig. 3.29), dung cake (Fig. 3.30) and husk (Fig. 3. 31).

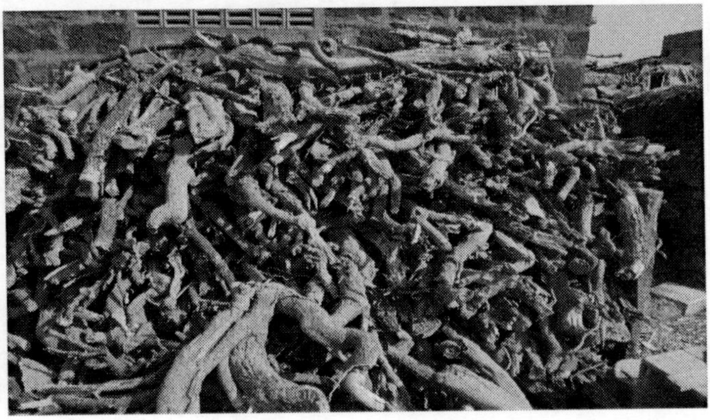

Fig. 3.29, woods

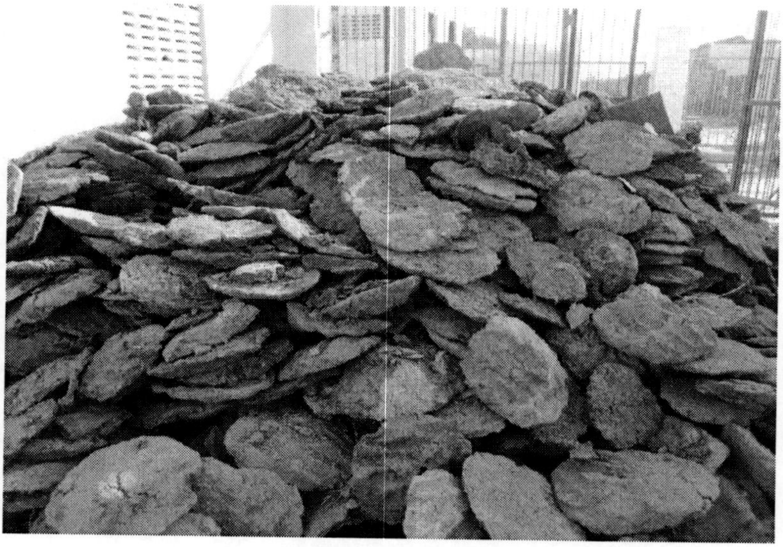

Fig. 3.30, dung cakes

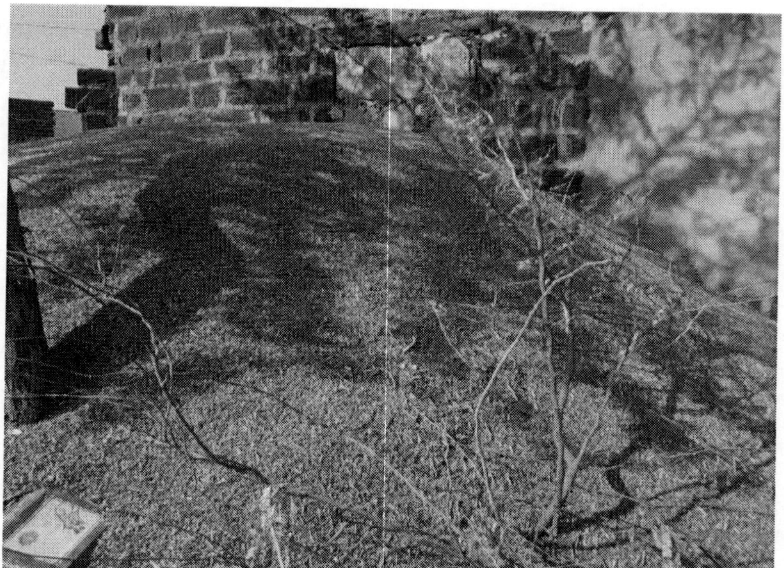

Fig. 3.31, husk

At 'Pokaran', this open kiln is locally known as 'aawa'. In a single 'aawa', costs about Rs. 10,000.00 of capital investment for the raw materials, but the profit they make by selling their commodity is very nominal.

In this method, a pit is dug on a plain ground upto a depth of 40 cm. In a simplest form it can be described that, pots are baked wither on a flat ground or in a pit. After the pit is dug, it is covered up with dung cakes and woods. This fuel is prepared and is raised a bit above the ground. In a 'aawa' 200 to 300 pots can be arranged along with other articles. After the fuel bed is ready, the pots are all arranged in a circular pattern around the kiln and the pots are all placed on one another in ascending order in inverted form, i.e., big pots are arranged below the small pots. Gap is maintained at regular interval of each pots. Those gaps are filled up with dry straws. After the pots have been arranged the piling process is completed. Then the entire dome structure is covered up with the broken pieces of pots and packed with dry husks. Further packing is done by plastering it with ash and mud. In this way the entire 'aawa' is sealed. One thing is to be noticed that fire channels are provided at the bottom. Each 'aawa' have one or two fire channels 'naali'. Through this fire channel fires are ignited. The fires are also pushed with a bamboo through this channel and in this way fires are reached at the centre of the fuel bed. Once the fire is set in, it is further bated by adding more fuel through those channel until the combustion process is completed. In this method the pots are all heated upto a temperature of 1200°C. This entire process of baking taken six days. First day took for the preparation, fire takes another one day to spread all around the 'aawa'. For the following two days the fire continue the combustion process and then the remaining dayswill take for cooling down. The pile is dismantled on the last day.

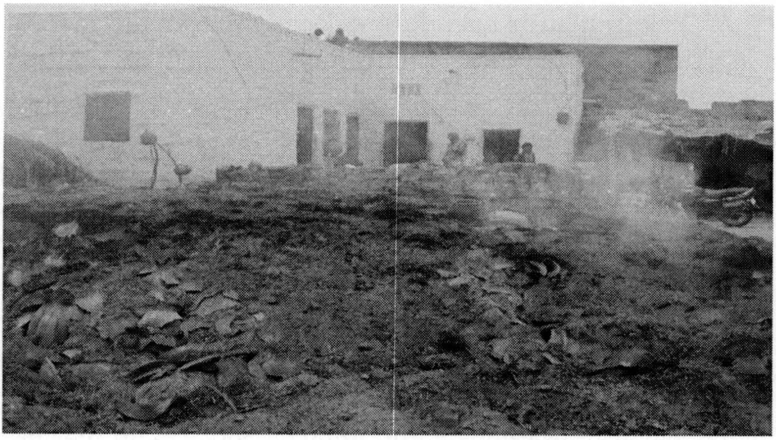

Fig. 3.32, baking of pottery in 'aawa'

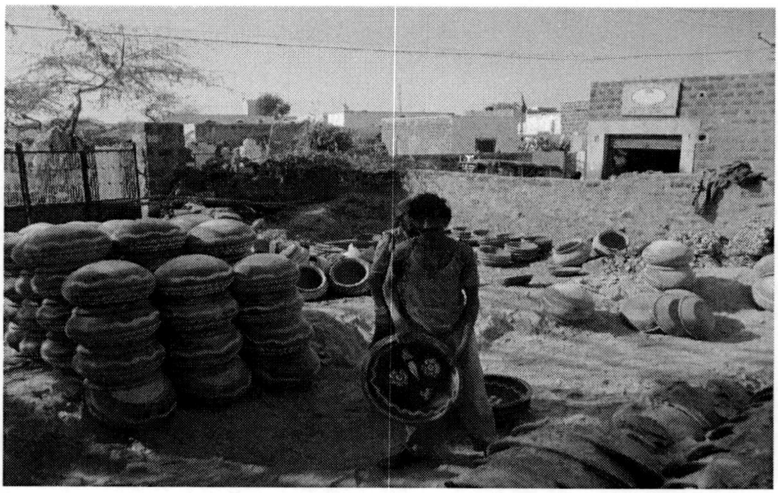

Fig. 3.33, potter removing the baked pots from the 'aawa'

AFTER FIRING TREATMENT

After the firing is completed it is often seen that some of the articles and pots get cracked. So it needs further treatment and repairing before selling it to the market.

It is observed in 'Molela' that sometimes due to excessive heat, the terracotta plaques get cracked and also broken into pieces. So, the cracks are all filled up with an adhesive made by mixing brick dust, adhesive and water in the ratio of 3:2:1. In the mixing process first of all brick are all turned into dust with a stone piece. Then the brick dust is put into a container or a cup and strong adhesive like fevicol is added into it (Fig. 3.35). When fevicol was not invented, traditionally they used lac for this purpose. Further water is added and thoroughly mixes it until and unless the solution is prepared. After preparing the solution, the potter takes out the broken pieces of plaques and applies the adhesive on the broken part (Fig. 3.36). In the same manner on another part adhesive is also applied and then both the parts are joined together. In case of filling up of minor cracks the mixture adhesive is pushed inside the gap and left it dry for some time (Fig. 3.37). Before the application of the mixture the surface of the plaque is smoothen by rubbing gently with a flat stone.

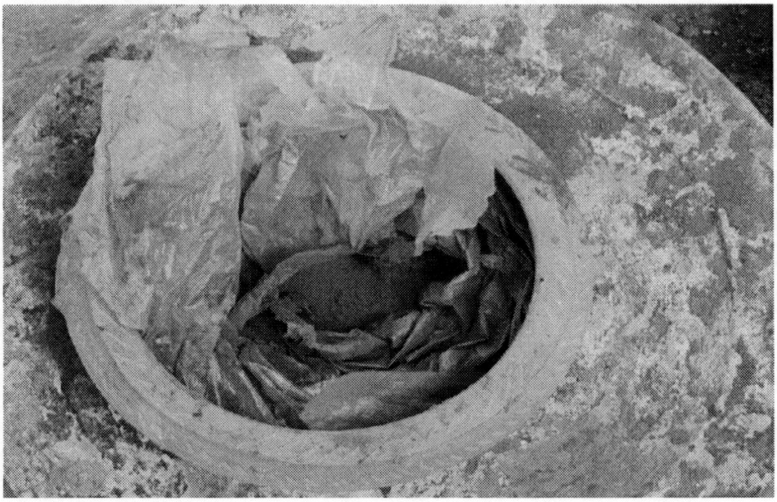

Fig. 3.34, brick dust

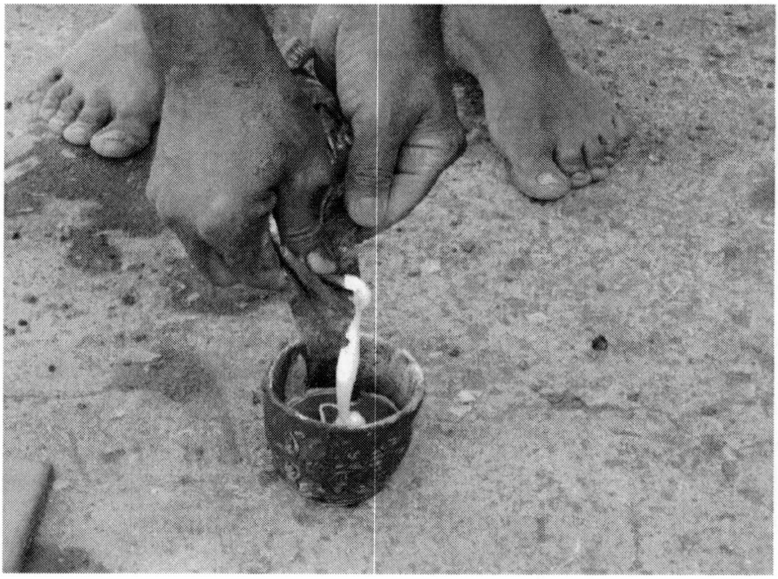

Fig. 3.35, adhesive is being added into the brick dust

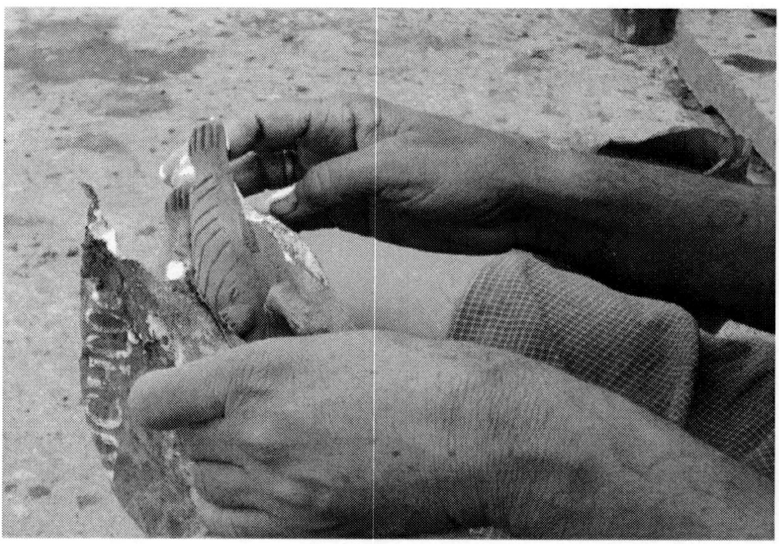

Fig. 3.36, potter applying adhesive for joining the broken parts

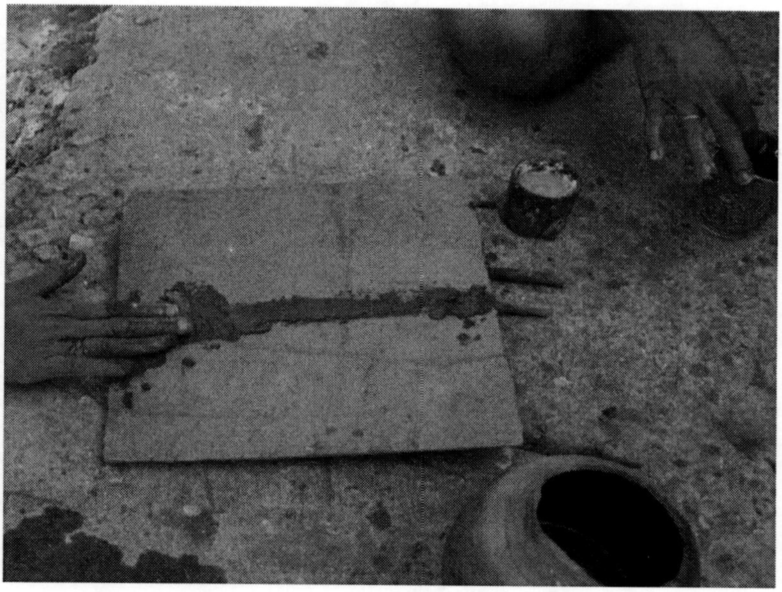

Fig. 3.37, filling up of cracks

After the crack is refilled and dried up they apply a slip made by mixing brick dust, glue and water in a light solution manner and apply it on both the surfaces of the terracotta plaque in order to cover the crake marks that have been repaired. The repaired parts are then put under the sun before giving it a finishing touch.

Apart from all these traditional methods discussed above the present potters also adopted some modern methods and applications too, such as, now a days electric wheel is being used in case of traditional wheel. The use of traditional wheel is get limited to some of the old potters because balancing is very much important while using traditional wheel as it rotate upon a single nail. Present generation are getting all the modern equipment in their hand. Electric wheel does not require balancing and maintaining of speed. It can be easily operated.

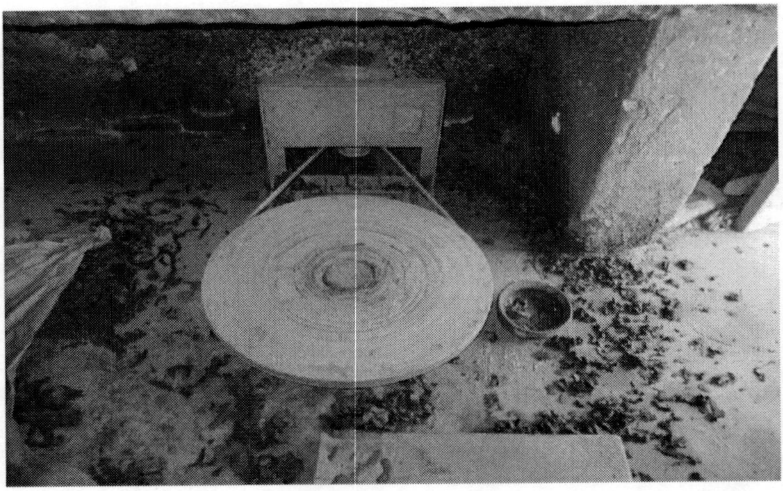

Fig. 3.38, electric wheel

As a whole it can be said, that in both the field areas the practise of traditional knowledge is still maintained by the potters somehow or other with a little adaptation of modern innovations.

5

PRODUCTS AND MARKETIZATION

A product is not at all a product if it is not marketized and a market cannot be called as market if it lacks product. So product and market are inseparable from each other. Here, this chapter begins with the products of 'Molela' and then with 'Pokaran'. Gradually the chapter will describe all the main products which are specified for each of the particular region. Marketization of product is also equally valuable. Hence, this chapter also not missed out this topic.

The traditional occupation of Molela potters are preparing the votive terracotta plaques of various ethnic deities along with the gods and goddesses of Hindu main stream. They generally produce this for their tribal customers. Their main customers are the tribals like Bhil, Garasiya, Sahariya, etc. who maintained this tradition and keep this traditional art alive. In the month of 'Magh', 'Kartik' and 'Baisak' according to the Hindu calendar, the tribes use to come and take their terracotta idols. But the season of festive and of best selling is 'Magh'. During this month of January, the tribal people use to come from distance places as far as Gujarat, Madhya Pradesh and from the other regions of Rajasthan by bus, train and even by foot to Molela to purchase their votive. The tribal people prefer brightly coloured terracotta plaques of various deities to take them away for their local shires and temples. They generally change their votives every year. Hence, when they come they choose the colour for painting and the potters paint it in front of them according to their direction. These people use to come in groups or single accompanied by a 'bhopa'. The 'bhopas' are generally the priests who perform all the ritual practises. To be more specified the 'bhopas' are some sort of 'tantrik' who practises totems. But 'bhopas' hold a very prestigious position in their village society. An interesting feature is noticed that, a single person can have his own 'bhopa', a family can possess a 'bhopa', a society can have their own 'bhopa' and even an entire village can nominate their own 'bhopa'. After the purchase, the payment is made by cash, grains, cloths, lands, etc., but now a days cash payment is most preferable. The 'bhopa' then carry the votive plaque on their head and take it to their respective place.

According to Jane Perryman "there are three levels of worship for a Hindu: at the temple, at the local shrine and within the household area at home. Clay vessels and oil lamps may be used as a part of ritual worship in temples but the offerings of terracotta is not a custom. Each village has shrines of its own patron deity, each caste group has shrines to its own preferred gods and there are family shrines dedicated to ancestors. The Hindu religion allows individuals to worship god and goddess of their own choice, so throughout India there are literally many millions of different gods. These deities may be linked to formal religion but are usually associated with the earth, fertility, agriculture and healing as well as the forces of nature. Worship revolves round the offering of terracotta figurines either to appease the god or to fulfil a vow in return for the favour."

Among the terracotta idols produced, the most popular one is the 'Dharmaraj'. He is also known as 'Devnarayan'. The people of Molela as well as the tribalsuse to worship this deity. On a plaque he is shown painted orange in the skin, a long moustache with beard, wearing large ear rings and brightly coloured striped dress. He is shown riding on a horse and holding a spear in his hand and adorned with jewellery. There is a believe in the village that, he is the god of justice. During night time he guard the entire village by riding on his horse and shoed away all evil spirits. 'Dharmaraj' is also regarded as a Rajput hero. Apart from 'Dharmaraj', there are other legendary heroes also which the people of Molela and surrounding villages use to worship and the potters use to make their idols. Such legendary heroes are 'Tejaji', 'Pabuji', 'Bhoonaji' and so on. They are all once a Rajput hero. During the course of my field work, I found mention of twenty five ethnic deities whose idols the Molela potters use to make and sell it to the people who worship those deities. The names are as follows and the descriptions of some of them along with the photographs are also furnished later.

Molela Deities:

1. Dharmaraj
2. Kala/ gora (Bheruji)
3. Kalika Mata
4. Pabuji
5. Takaji
6. Suhar Baba
7. Gokaji
8. Radaji
9. Ganeshji
10. Rebari
11. Umba Mata

12. Chamunda Mata
13. Husti Mata
14. Macchi Mata
15. Hansa Mata
16. Sand Mata
17. Nagni Mata
18. Suar Mata
19. Awaj Mata
20. Pipalaj
21. Kokra Mata
22. Panch Devi
23. Durga Mata
24. Niyaji
25. Phwarji

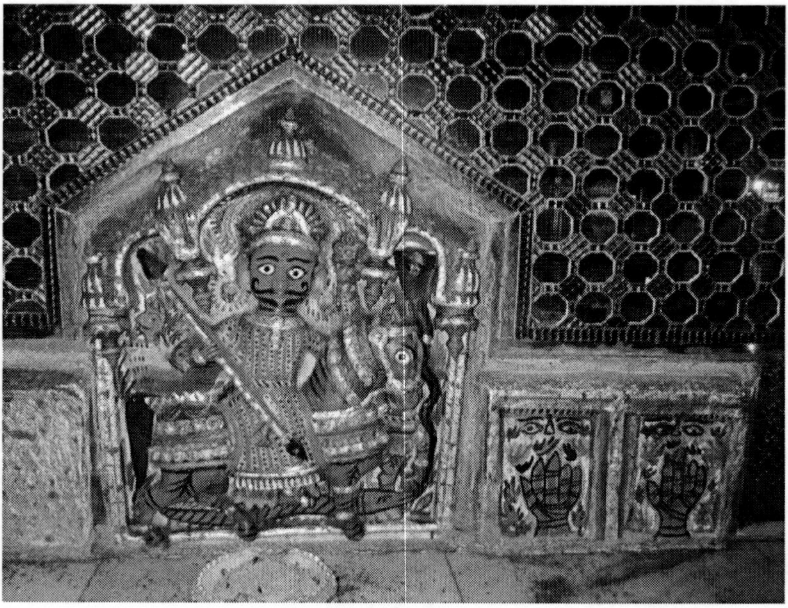

Fig. 4.1, Dharmaraj

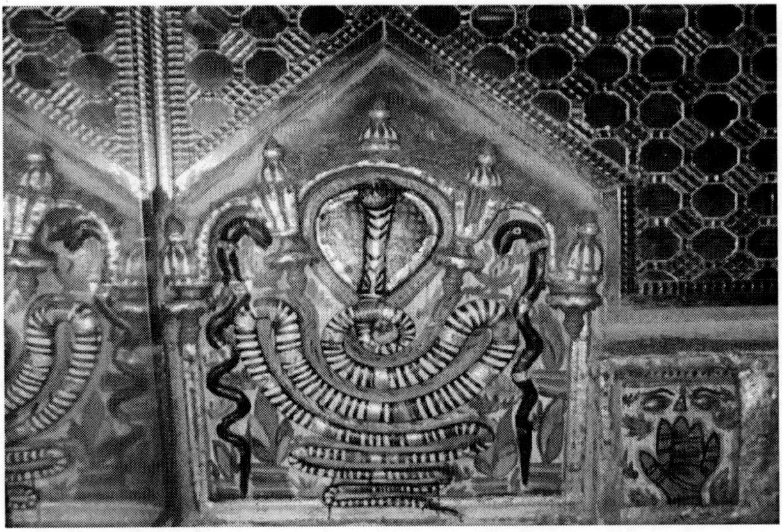

Fig. 4.2, Nagadeva

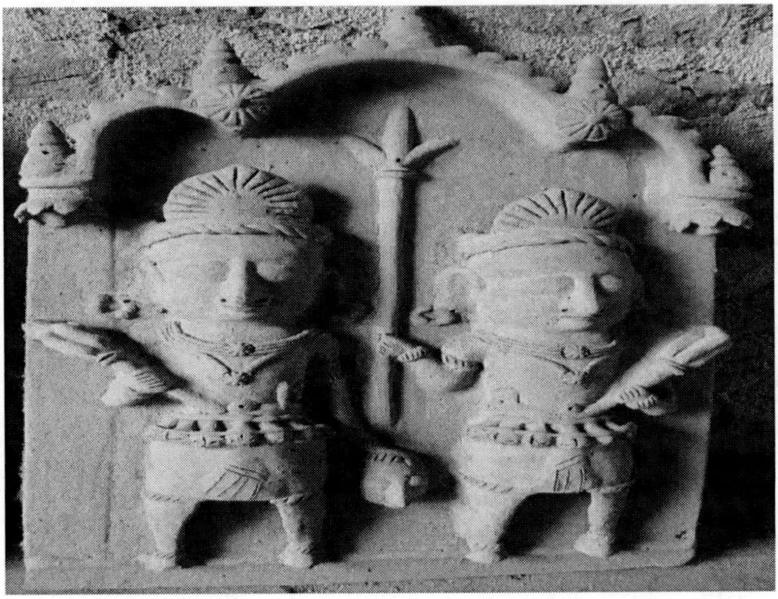

Fig. 4.3, an unfinished plaque of 'Bheruji'

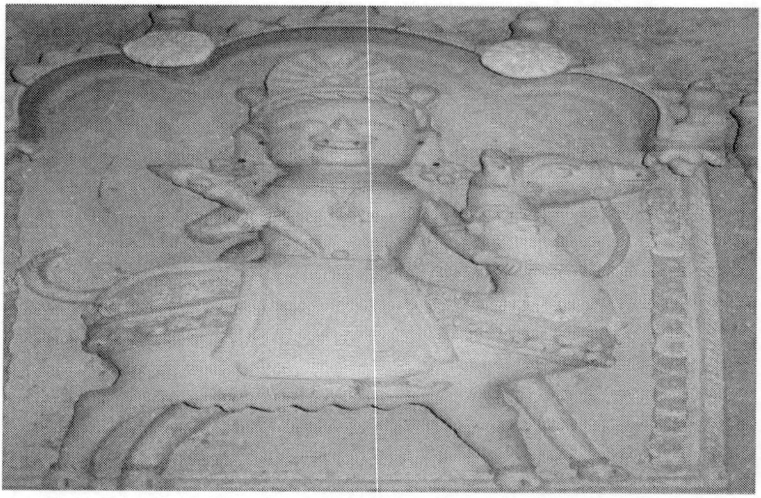

Fig. 4.4, Rebari

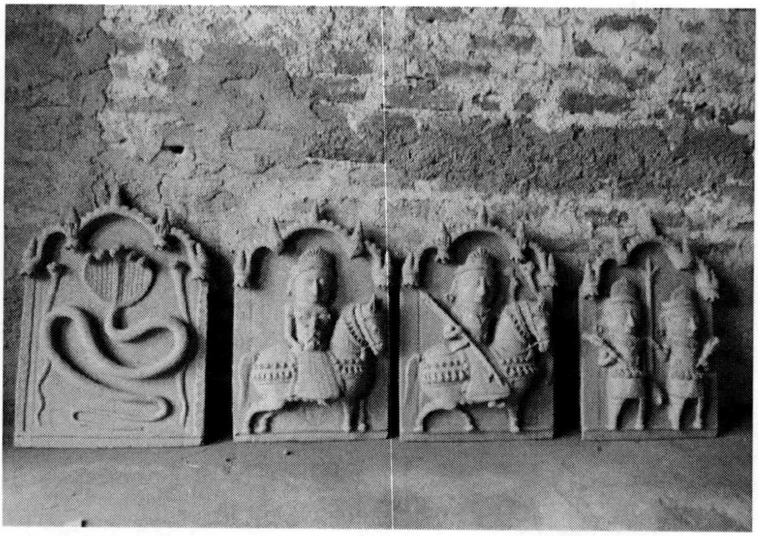

Fig. 4.5, unfinished terracotta plaques of local deities

'Bheruji' is also known as 'Kala- Gora' is worshiped by the Molela people. One of the potter informed that, 'Kala' is cunning and accept non- veg offerings and liquor. Whereas 'Gora' is calm and accept sweet offerings such as fruits and vegetables. There as certain deities which are worshiped by some specific group of people only and they come to purchase their votive from the potter. For example, 'Uuth Mata' and 'Rebari' is worship by the 'Rebari' community of people. This deity symbolises their dependency on camel. They are the herdsmen and use to domesticate camel. 'Sand Mata' is worship by the 'Dangi'. 'Singha Mata' is worshiped by the 'Rajputs'. 'Kalka Mata' and 'Bheruji' is worshiped by 'Gadoliya Lohar'.

Many organisation and personnel played their prominent role to promote this craft and subsequently to promote this industry. There is also a question raised that, how 'Molela' became famous? The answers to this question are as follows:

Traditionally the potters of 'Molela' makes the votive idols for their tribal customers and for the other communities which is prevalent till today. But in the year 1979, Sri Jyotindra Jain, the then Director of Handicraft Board of India, New Delhi visited Molela. He then directed the potters to make something different apart from those traditional votive images. The new innovations consists of the plaques and tiles depicting their daily village activity, their social life, their way of living, as a whole representing the entire picture of village life. Stories from 'Ramayana' and 'Mahabharata', historical events (Fig. 4.6) are all shown on their terracotta tiles. This method brings a new dimension to their art and makes the people to think in a new way.As a result of this new conception they came on focus. Their sellings also increase. Demands from the outside market also comes. At our present stage of knowledge, now much more varieties comes. They also adopted many art patterns from other regions such as 'Pokaran', 'Jaipur', 'Bikaner', etc. They are producing wide variety of articles apart from their traditional one. The other varieties of articles include crockery, terracotta toys, diwali lamps, pottery of various types such as flower pots, flower vase of embossed pattern which are use as decorative purposes. Crockery includes black ware (Fig. 4.7) and curd bowl are made for store milk and curd, 'kundi', a wide mouthed shallow bowl for keeping chapatti, most common water pots which are sold in the local market, ghee pot shown human face, the thin neck and rim give elegance to the form, incense holder, tribal wine bottle etc. 'Takhmal – 28' is a art group of Rajasthan. They organise national terracotta camp on 1081 at Molela. 'Aaj' is another art group also encouraged the modern artists. In the year 1984, Sri Gaganbihari Dadaich, Lecturer at Nathdwara Govt. College play a pioneer role. Till now he is actively working for the upliftment of this art. He is also taking many measures and encouraging young potters in order to promote this traditional handicraft and to conserve our heritage.

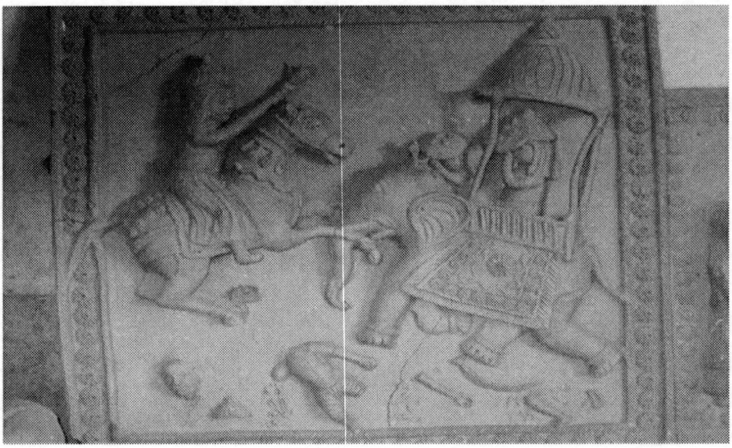

Fig. 4.6, plaque showing the historical event of the battle of MaharanaPratap with the Raja Man Singh of Jaipur in the battle of Haldighati

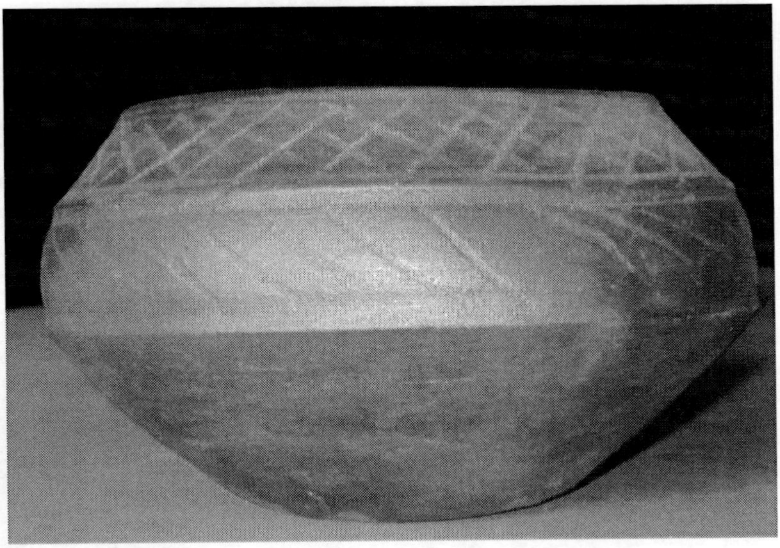

Fig. 4.7, Black Ware

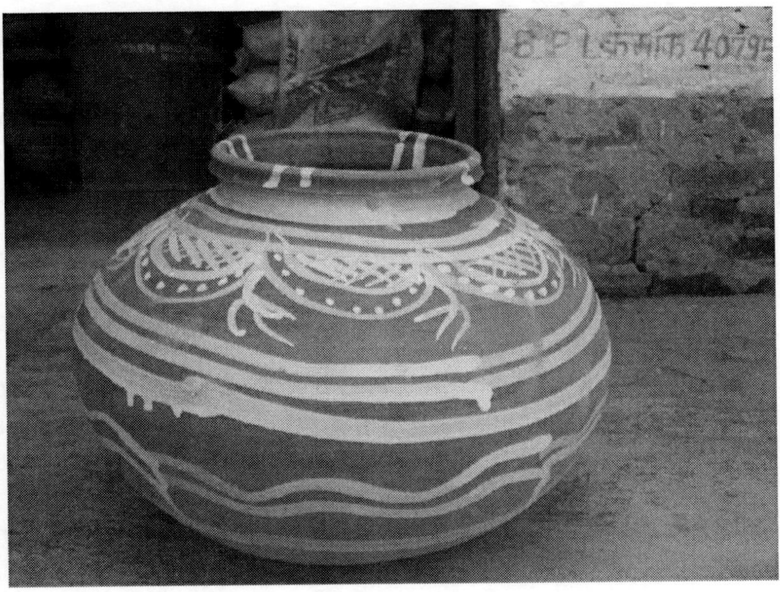

Fig. 4.8, painted water pot

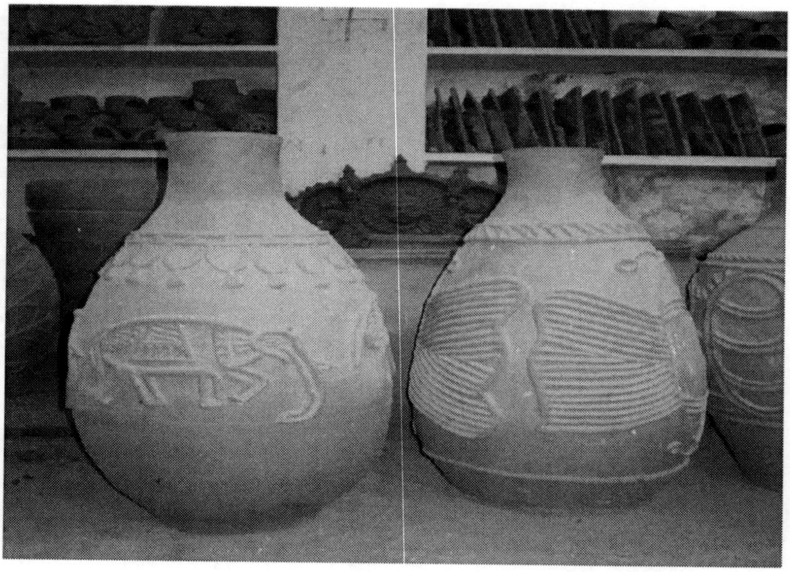

Fig. 4.9, flower vase with emboss pattern on the surface

The small crockery and diwali lamps are generally sold in the local market and surrounding villages, but the terracotta tile works depicting various floral and faunal images, pictures, patterns, decorative articles and big size plaques are all made by special order. Those articles are sold in whole sale and carried by middle men or contractors and are transported to distance places and other states. Often those are also exported to foreign countries.

During the time of big festivals like 'Ganesh Chaturthi' and 'Dusheera' they also get special order for the idols of Lord Ganesha and Durga. People from other districts and states also visit Molela to purchase those idols. Prices are all fixed according to the demand and supply of the product. The size and weight of the product also influence the transportation cost and thus price is accordingly. In case of the terracotta plaques, the plaques are all arranged in a card board box and packed it before transporting them.

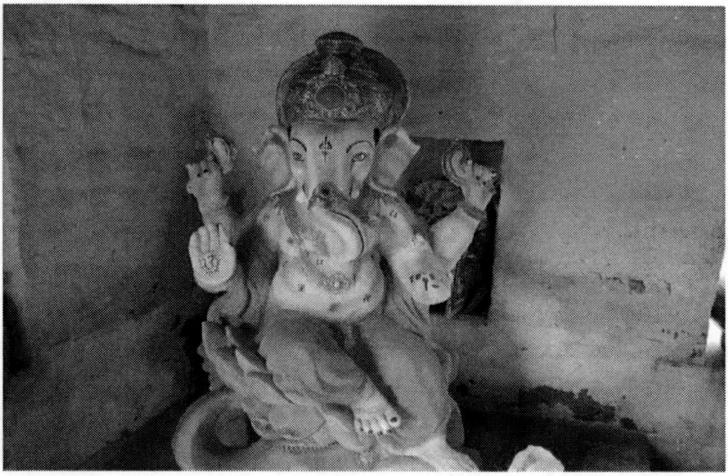

Fig. 4.10, idol of Ganesha is prepared for the occasion of 'Ganesh Chaturthi'

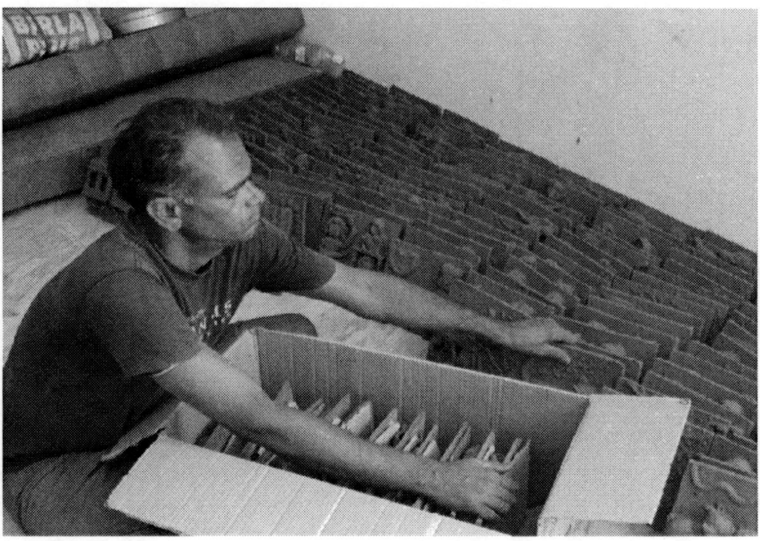

Fig. 4.11, packing of terracotta plaques for the market

Another step is taken by 'Takhmal- 28'. This organisation organised National Terracotta Camp in the year 1981 at Molela to encourage the young generation about their traditional terracotta art. On this occasion the artist from all over India was invited to demonstrate their art. Another art group known as 'Aaj', also played a vital role.

Apart from all these above mentioned measurements taken by those institutions and organisation there are also number of potters who makes this 'Molela Art' famous. Many national and international award winners are present in the village. Some of them also visited abroad like Europe, America, Australia, etc. to demonstrate their art. The detail activities of some of the potters are as follows :

Jamnalal Kumhar

Award Received: 1988-89- Udaipur District Award

1988-89- Rajasthan State Award

1994-95- Rajsamand District Award

Demonstration:

And Exhibition: 1988- Demonstration at Gujarat Vidhyapeth Organised by Heritage Trust at Bhuvan School, Baroda.

1988- Terracotta exhibition and sale at Seth House, KhelMaidan, New Delhi.

1989- Shaskriti, Jamnalal Bajaj Bhawan, Bombay.

1989- Council of Advancement of People's Action and Rural Technology, (WZCC), Udaipur.

1991- Market Meet, display exhibition and demonstration at Jaipur.

1991- Gawalior Trade Fair.

1992- Contemporary Arts and Crafts at Ellish Bridge, Ahmedabad.

1993- Rajasthan Pavilion at PragatiMaidan, New Delhi.

1993- WZCC at Shilpagram Udaipur.

1994- Exhibition at Faculty of Fine Arts at M.S. University, Baroda.

1995- World Wide Fund for Nature, India.

1999- TradicniIndickaTerrakota: Parah, Czech Republic.

2002- The Academy of Fine Arts Prague, Czech Republic.

2003- -do-

2004- FridaSteinburger, Israel.

2006- -do-

2008- MaharanaMewar Charitable Foundation, Udaipur.

2009- WZCC, Udaipur.

2010- National Institute of Design, Ahmedabad.

2010- Jawahar Kala Kendra, Jaipur.

2011- Art College, Goa.

2011- Indubhai Parekh School of Architecture, Rajkot.

Mukesh Prajapat

Award Received: 2007-10- Society for International Language.

2009- DIC Award Terracotta.

2009- Wager- MewarPrajapat Society, Udaipur.

Demonstration:

And Exhibition: 2005- Exhibition of Molela Terracotta, Baroda.

2007- Society of International Language at Molela.

2009- DIC and State Handicraft Board Exhibition, Jaipur.

2009- Rajasthan Craft Mela, Jaipur.

2009- Shilpagram Festival, Udaipur.

2011- Workshop on Protecting Craft Indications Through G.I., Molela.

2011- Participate in 14th International Ceramic Festival, Arthous, France.

Shyamlal Kumhar

Demonstration:

And Exhibition: 1997- Faculty of Fine Arts, Baroda.

1998- Demonstration at Gujarat Vidhyapeth Organised by Heritage Trust at Bhuvan School, Baroda.

1991- WZCC, Udaipur.

1992- Gawalior Trade Fair.

1993- Craft Mela of NZCC, Chandigarh.

1997- All India Traditional Art Camp, Jaipur.

1998- DIC and State Handicraft Board Exhibition, Jaipur.

2007- One month demonstration camp at Jaipur.

2011- International Terracotta camp organised by Studio 25 Terra- Cotta at Molela. 2011- Participate in 14th International Ceramic Festival, Arthous, France.

So, due to this joint efforts of many Government and Non- Government organisations, individual efforts and hard work of potters make this small village popular. Earlier, it was not so much popular and was limited upto the surrounding areas. This rich art was caught by the eyes of enthusiasts which led to its popularization. The potters also use to visit time to time at the exhibitions organise around India. There they use to demonstrate and sell their articles. Apart from it, many small and large scale measurements are also taken time to time to promote this art. Hence, it can be said that it's a combined effort which makes this traditional handicraft to come under the light of exposure.

The potters of Pokaran are well known for their exclusive pottery. Traditionally they are not famous for terracotta work like that of Molela but they are expertise in making wide range of pottery that are regularly use for domestic and ritual purposes. They use to make both big size and small size pots. Big size potteries are 'chada', 'bhani', 'ghara', etc. The names of the important potteries are 'chada', 'pariya', 'tawniyan', 'kuldi', 'ghara', 'matka', 'tambena', 'lota', 'handi', 'parat'. 'Ghara', 'matka' and 'tambena' are used for store water. Water is drawn out with 'lota'. 'Lota' is also useful for drinking water. Such kind of pictures can be seen in rural India. The villagers never use glass like that of urban people.

Curd is prepared and store in 'handi'. 'Parat' is designed for kneading flour and prepare curd from milk. 'Chada' is use for churning purposes to churn out butter from the milk. Then the extracted butter is kept in 'pariya' or 'tawniyan'. Later on the butter is heated in these vessels to transform it into ghee. And at last the ghee is finally stored in 'kuldi'. 'Kuldi' is the smallest of all vessels. So, the above mentioned discussion clearly showed the functions of each vessel in daily life and how they associated with each other.

Apart from all these household articles the potters also manufacture many decorative pottery such as designing flower vase, pots, etc. 'Bhani' is also a type of decorative pot.

All the above mentioned household vessels are generally

sold in the local market of Pokaran, Ramdeora and at Jaisalmer which is 105 km away from Pokaran. The village people themselves use those. Chada and parat are mostly sold. These articles are mainly sold by lot to the desert villages of Barmer, Bikaner, Jodhpur and Jaisalmer. Such commodities have a good market in the above mentioned districts. These are transported by truck through agent. Decorative articles such as terracotta tiles, toys, animal figurines, etc. are both sold in the local market as well as exported. Apart from it there are also some articles which are made by special order. Generally their customers are the big hotel owners, bunglows and the army men.

In Pokaran an organisation named 'Kumhar Hasthakala Vikas Samiti' was established on 23rd May 2003 in collaboration with 'Rural Non Farm Development Agency, Jaipur' with the aim and objective for the progress and development of potters and their art. This organisation was also set up for giving training to the women in order to encourage the cottage industry. But unlike 'Molela' the potters of 'Pokaran' did not get that level of exposure.

6

ABOUT THE COMMUNITY AND THEIR PRESENT STATUS

Saraswati and Behura has described the nomenclature of so called potters community as "excepting in Kashmir Valley, where they are called 'karal', in the whole of western, central, northern and eastern India the potters are known as 'kumhar or 'kumbhar'. In West Bengal, the potters are also referred to as 'kumor'.

In southern India, they are called 'kusavan' in Tamil; 'kusavan' or 'kuyarvan' in Malayalam; 'kuvara' or 'kumbara' in Kanarese, 'kusave' in Tulu; and 'kummara' or 'kumrulu' in Telugu. Etymologically, all these names have been derived from the original Sanskrit word 'kumbhakara', 'pot maker'. In parts of Western Orissa, potters are also known as 'Bhande' which is the derivation of the Sanskrit word 'bhanda', a pot." Apart from this nomenclature, the potters regarded themselves as the son of Lord Brahma who is the creator of this earth. Their justification behind this statement is that, as Brahma has created this earth with the combination of mud and water, similarly they are also use to create object with mud and water which we all called as pot. After surveying among the potter community of both the fields some important findings came into forefront.

The Kumhars of Molela are broadly divided into two groups viz. 'Mewliya' and 'Mewara'. Terracotta works of making votive idols are actually associated with the Mewliyas, whereas pot making was associated with the Mewaras. But now a days both of them makes both these commodities. Mewara kumhar came from outside and Mewliyas are the original settlers. This is a controversy theory. Mewara and Mewliya are the two brothers. Mewliyas were actually Mewara in the beginning, but later on they became separated. There is a historical story behind this.

The people who get married women are later became Mewliya. The tribal women are called as 'Mrinis'. When they get married with the 'Mrinis', they became 'Mewliya'. The women of Mewliya Kumhar use to wear nose ring (nath) and the Mewara women never wear such. Both of these groups get married among themselves. Interestingly, these two groups holds two different views and always try to establish their own authority. The Mewliyas hold that they are the original settlers of Molela and Mewaras come from the Mewar region of Rajasthan, hence were termed as 'Mewara'. On the other hand the Mewaras claiming that the Mewliya were actually the Mewaras and later on they became detached from their main part. Some potters state that all the kumhars of Molela get migrated from other regions like Nadol and Abrol and settled in Molela from time to time.

According to them, their ancestors came in Molela around 600- 700 years ago and started the art of terracotta and pottery making.

There is legendary story behind the origin of this community. Once there was a blind potter. One night he dreamt of 'Dharmaraj'. In his dream 'Dharmaraj' instructed him to make his idol and in the next morning he get back his sight.

After that the next generation adopted this profession. There are all total thirty six families of potter at Molela, but earlier it was about fifty. With the passage of time many of them left this job, some shifted to other place. The following tables associated with the total population of potters at the village, sex composition, marital status and educational status are all prepared after surveying in these thirty six households.

Table no. 1: Population and Sex Composition

Sl. No.	Age Group	Male	%	Female	%	Total	%
1	0-5	8	8.33	4	5.19	12	6.93
2	6-10	14	14.58	7	9.09	21	12.13
3	11-15	7	7.29	8	10.38	15	8.67
4	16-20	13	13.54	5	6.49	18	10.40
5	21-25	4	4.16	5	6.49	9	5.20
6	26-30	7	7.29	6	7.79	13	7.51
7	31-35	6	6.25	13	16.88	19	10.98
8	36-40	17	17.70	6	7.79	23	13.29
9	41-45	2	2.08	3	3.89	5	2.89
10	46-50	3	3.12	5	6.49	8	4.62
11	51-55	5	5.20	1	1.29	6	3.46
12	56-60	0	0	5	6.49	5	2.89
13	61-65	5	5.20	2	2.59	7	4.04
14	66-70	3	3.12	4	5.19	7	4.04
15	71+	2	2.08	3	3.89	5	2.89
		96	100.00	77	100.00	173	100.00

The above table shows that the total population of kumhars in Molela is 173 out of which 96 are male and 77 are female. The sex ratio of male is more as compared to female.

Table No. 2: Marital Status

Sl. No.	Marital Status	Male	%	Female	%	Total	%
1	Unmarried	49	51.04	23	29.87	72	41.62
2	Married	46	47.92	46	59.74	92	53.18
3	Widow	1	1.04	8	10.39	9	5.20
4	Divorced	0	0	0	0	0	0
	Total	96	100.00	77	100.00	173	100.00

The above table shows that, in the village of Molela, there are 49 unmarried male and 46 married male with that of one widow. As compared to female unmarried number is 23 and married is 46. However the number of widow is more than man in case of female. Hence, this table shows the total number of married persons are 92 and unmarried are 72 out of total population of 173.

Table No. 3: Male literacy rate

Sl. No.	Age Group	Illiterate	%	Literate	%
1	0-5	5	55.55	3	3.44
2	6-10	0	0	14	16.09
3	11-15	0	0	7	8.04
4	16-20	0	0	13	14.94
5	21-25	0	0	4	4.59
6	26-30	0	0	7	8.04
7	31-35	0	0	6	6.89
8	36-40	0	0	17	19.54
9	41-45	0	0	2	2.29
10	46-50	0	0	3	3.44
11	51-55	0	0	5	5.74
12	56-60	0	0	0	0

13	61-65	2	22.22	3	3.44
14	66-70	1	11.11	2	2.29
15	71+	1	11.11	1	1.14
	Total	9	100.00	87	100.00

The total percentage of illiterate male in Molela is 9.38 %. And literate is 90.63 %.

Table No. 4: Female literacy rate

Sl. No.	**Age Group**	**Illiterate**	**%**	**Literate**	**%**
1	0-5	2	6.25	2	4.44
2	6-10	0	0	7	15.55
3	11-15	0	0	8	17.77
4	16-20	0	0	5	11.11
5	21-25	0	0	5	11.11
6	26-30	0	0	6	13.33
7	31-35	6	18.75	7	15.55
8	36-40	3	9.37	3	6.66
9	41-45	2	6.25	1	2.22
10	46-50	5	15.62	0	0
11	51-55	1	3.12	0	0
12	56-60	4	12.5	1	2.22
13	61-65	2	6.25	0	0
14	66-70	4	12.5	0	0
15	71+	3	9.37	0	0
	Total	32	100.00	45	100.00

The total percentage of illiterate female in Molela is 41.56 %. And literate is 58.44 %.

The literacy rate of male is higher than female. But the illiterate female ismaximum in number.

The Mewliya kumhar belongs from 'Asawala' clan and the Mewara belongs from 'Sawliya' clan. Inter clan marriage is prohibited among them. Mewliyakumhars are majority in number. Although they belongs to Hindu religion and worship all Hindu deities, but they also have their own kuladevi. Mewara potters use to worship 'Sreyamata' and Mewliya use to worship 'Ashapura'. Nadol in Pali district have the temple of Ashapura. Mainly in Navaratri they use to visit. The potters belong from the OBC category.

Role of Kumhars in village social activity: from my long research work in this field, I noticed that, there are not so much interactions among the people. The village consists of many groups and sub groups and people from various caste and communities, but all are concerned about their own interest. Even among the potters also there are internal clash which is one of the prime reason for which the art is dying. On the day of festival, milk is collected from the entire village who have cows and buffaloes. From those milk 'kheer' is prepared and offered to the god. After the completion of the ceremony, the kheer is served to each and every houses of the entire village as a 'prasad'. The people are also use to gather at the temple to enjoy the feast. In this respect, the potters are assigned the task to collect milk and water from the village. They use to fetch the first milk early in the morning when the cattles are mulched. Those milk and water are brought in the pots prepared by the kumhars themselves. The kumhar serve those milk and water in the temple. This is the age old tradition which is continuing from the time immemorable. But now a days due to availability of water supply, tube wells, water tanker, the kumhars are no longer going to fetch water from the well or pond. This modern method they are adopted and that's why the tradition is changed. The lower caste people are generally avoided. The milk are not brought from the houses of lower caste people such as the tribes, chamars, dome, etc.

Rajputs, Brahmanas, Jains, Gairis are the suppliers of milk. On the day of festival, milk is not use for any other purpose. The caste system is still prevalent in the village Molela.

Apart from this yearly festival, Dharmaraj is worshipped on every Saturday and Khedamata on every Sunday. During these days also milk is brought and kheer is prepared. The 'Bhopas' are the religious priest. Bhopa can belong from any community.

He can be a Rajput, Brahman, Kumhar, Gamiti, etc. The tribals also have their own Bhopa. He has been regarded as an incarnation of Lord Dharmaraj. There is a belief that, Dharmaraj use to come inside the person who is a Bhopa and he will immediately start acting like Dharmaraj and remain in trans condition. That time he became a spiritual being. In this way next Bhopa is selected after the existing Bhopa. The people believe that, the Bhopa have the power to cure any diseases, remove evil spirits, epidemics and even venom from a snake bite effected person.

Apart from the village fairs and festivals the kumhars also have other roles. In marriage ceremonies the kumhars are assigned the task of fetching and serving water. But presently stage, this tradition is also vanishing due to availability of easy modern water supply facilities. Earlier the kumhar use to fetch water and serve those to the guests and in return they receive a share of two or three bags of grains, cloths, share of food and cash payment also according to their demands and requirements. In village festivals, marriage and other social ceremonies, the lower castes are assigned the task of cleaning of utensils, sweeping and Sutars use to bring wood for fuel. They also do the work of carpentry, making of to ranas (gate), etc. in this way different communities play their own role in village life. Such type of social bonding are there in the early village society, but now slowly- slowly all such traditions are changing. Now the people are very much concerned about their own interest and they want to come out from all such social bondings.

In my next field at Pokaran, I surveyed around ninety eight families of potter and prepared the following findings in a table format. Analysis of data is also done. The story about the Pokaran potters is that they are carrying out their tradition from generation after generation. The Rajput rulers and Thakurs bring them long back at Pokaran and settled them to satisfy their need. They were appointed for the job of utensil making. For cooking and ritual purposes utensils are needed. That's why the kumhars are brought from different regions of Rajasthan to make all those articles. With the progress of time they became the settlers of Pokaran. The Pokaranpotters belong from 'Branna' clan and comes under OBC category.

Table No. 5: Population and sex composition

Sl. No.	Age Group	Male	%	Female	%	Total	%
1	0-5	32	10.99	44	17.25	76	13.91
2	6-10	42	14.43	32	12.54	74	13.55
3	11-15	41	14.08	25	9.80	66	12.08
4	16-20	34	11.68	35	13.72	69	12.63
5	21-25	32	10.99	25	9.80	57	10.43
6	26-30	31	10.65	19	7.45	50	9.15
7	31-35	16	5.49	15	5.88	31	5.67
8	36-40	9	3.09	15	5.88	24	4.39
9	41-45	13	4.46	9	3.52	22	4.02
10	46-50	9	3.09	8	3.13	17	3.11
11	51-55	9	3.09	7	2.74	16	2.93
12	56-60	5	1.71	10	3.92	15	2.74

13	61-65	6	2.06	4	1.56	10	1.83
14	66-70	7	2.40	3	1.17	10	1.83
15	71+	5	1.71	4	1.56	9	1.64
	Total	291	100.00	255	100.00	546	100.00

The total population of male potters in Pokaran is 291 which is comparatively high of the female population of 255 out of 546.

Table No. 6: Marital status

Sl. No.	Marital Status	Male	%	Female	%	Total	%
1	Unmarried	148	50.86	105	41.18	253	46.34
2	Married	139	47.77	140	54.90	279	51.10
3	Widow	4	1.37	10	3.92	14	2.56
4	Divorced	0	0	0	0	0	0
	Total	291	100.00	255	100.00	546	100.00

By looking into the table of marital status it is found that the total percentage of unmarried male is 50.86% and female is 41.18%. Similarly the percentage of married male is 47.77% and female is 54.90%. Hence, the total married population is 279 and out of 546 of total population of potters at Pokaran.

Table No. 7: Male literacy rate

Sl. No.	Age Group	Illiterate	%	Literate	%
1	0-5	29	43.28	3	1.33
2	6-10	3	4.47	39	17.41
3	11-15	2	2.98	39	17.41
4	16-20	1	1.49	33	14.73
5	21-25	2	2.98	30	13.39

6	26-30	4	5.97	27	12.05
7	31-35	2	2.98	14	6.25
8	36-40	3	4.47	6	2.67
9	41-45	2	2.98	11	4.91
10	46-50	4	5.97	5	2.23
11	51-55	1	1.49	8	3.57
12	56-60	2	2.98	3	1.33
13	61-65	4	5.97	2	0.89
14	66-70	4	5.97	3	1.33
15	71+	4	5.97	1	0.44
	Total	67	100.00	224	100.00

Table No. 8: Female literacy rate

Sl. No.	Age Group	Illiterate	%	Literate	%
1	0-5	42	33.07	2	1.56
2	6-10	4	3.14	28	21.87
3	11-15	1	0.78	24	18.75
4	16-20	11	8.66	24	18.75
5	21-25	6	4.72	19	14.84
6	26-30	8	6.29	11	8.59
7	31-35	7	5.51	8	6.25
8	36-40	9	7.08	6	4.68
9	41-45	7	5.51	2	1.56
10	46-50	6	4.72	2	1.56
11	51-55	6	4.72	1	0.78
12	56-60	9	7.08	1	0.78
13	61-65	4	3.14	0	O
14	66-70	3	2.36	0	0

15	71+	4	3.14	0	0
	Total	127	100.00	128	100.00

After analysing the above mentioned table the total percentage of illiterate men comes 23.02%. and women 49.80 %. Whereas the literacy rate is concerned, 76.98 % of men are literate and 50.20 % of women are literate.

Inter relation with the other Community

Potters traditionally known as 'kumhara' are pan Indian community. While describing about the inter relation with the other communities it is obvious that they have to depend on other for selling their products and similarly other has also to depend on them to buy the clay articles from them to for the ritual and domestic purposes. Examples may be given of Molela potters that, they use to make the terracotta votives for their tribal and non tribal customers. Hence, it can be said that, the potters are maintaining their religious believes and simultaneously the tribals also supporting their economic life. Another point is that, the potters use to bring the donkey dung from the grazing ground situated in the Kalbelia area. The Kalbelia generally domesticate the donkeys. The Kalbelias also often sell the donkey dung to the potters. They generally charge Rs. 100.00 per bag (bori). The charge also depend upon the need of money for the Kalbelia on the basis of demand and supply. The gum 'dawrigund' which is use by the Molela potters to mix with colour are brought by the tribal people. They use to purchase it from them @ Rs. 400.00 or 500.00 per kilo. Often the potters also visit Gogunda in Udaipur district in order to purchase those gum. On the another field at Pokaran, noticed the same inter relation with little variations. For example, the potters of Pokaran often purchase the mineral pigments from the Muslims. The dung cakes for the fuel are brought from Khetolai, 25 km away from Pokaran.

Those dung cakes are supplied by the Bishnoi community of people. Apart from all these above mention examples there are also certain points which are noticed which seems to be a minute factor by carries a great significance, such as the tools which the potter use are also made by others. The tools which are wooden made are made by the 'Sutars'. The iron implements are prepared by the 'GadoliyaLohar'. In this way they maintain their inter relation.

Present Status

Economically seen the kumhars live on subsistence level and any bearing any big and extra expenditure quite tough for them. So, the Government have recommended them under the category of Other Backward Classes. The reverse side of the coin has presented a sad picture. It was observed at Molela that the present generation are not taking any interest to take up this art as a profession. They are simple leaving this job. There are various factors such as shortage of raw materials specially soil crisis, increasing price in fuel and transportation, competition in the market and disunity among the potters has threatened the existence of this craft. The amount they receive after selling their product is very nominal. It not at all satisfies their labour and other investment. The difference between Molela status and Pokaran status is that ay Molela the potters are facing the availability of raw materials mainly the clay. But their product have a good market value. Whereas in Pokaran, there are abundance of raw materials. They are not facing the shortage for the supply of clay, wood, husk, straw, dungs, etc. but the market is not up to that level of satisfaction. In general for all potters that they are leaving the job because one of the prime factor is that, the fragmentation of land among the family members.

Hence, they are facing the space crisis. They are not

getting enough space to set up kiln, storing and drying of products and raw materials. "Change is inevitable brought about by economic and social pressures in a time of political and industrial development. But it is pity that the old should be stigmatised for the wrong reasons as being primitive, and the social status should depend on the destruction of what was beautiful and precious." Jane Perryman.

BIBLIOGRAPHY

Chaudhuri, P. 2011- 'Pokhran Potters of Shilpagram', Journal of the Anthropological Survey of India, Vol. 60. No. 1 (pp. 147- 150)

Chaudhuri, P. 2011- 'A Cursory Look into the Terracotta Objects in Molela- A Rajasthan Village', Journal of the Anthropological Survey of India, Vol. 60. No. 2 (pp. 321-324)

Chattopadhyay, K. 1985- Handicrafts of India. New Delhi: Indian Council for Cultural Relations.

Gupta, M. 2004- Rajasthan Jeelewar Sanaskritik Avm Aytihasik Adhyaan. Vol. 1. Rajasthani Granthagar, Jodhpur.

Gupta, M. 2004- Rajasthan Jeelewar Sanaskritik Avm Aytihasik Adhyaan. Vol. 2. Rajasthani Granthagar, Jodhpur.

Meena, B.R. and Tripathi, A. 2001- 2002- 'Excavations at Ojiyana: A Unique Copper Age Site in Aravalli', Pragdhara 12: 45- 66.

Misra, V.N. 1967- Pre- and Proto- history of the Berach Basin, South Rajasthan. Poona: Deccan College, Research Institute.

Mookherjee, A. 1986- Folk Art of India. New Delhi: Clarion Books.

Pal, H. B. 1984- Handicrafts of Rajasthan. New Delhi: Publications Division.

Perryman, J. Traditional Potters of India. A & C Black- London.

Prakash, S. and Srivastava, V. S. 1981- Cultural Contours of India. Abhinav Publications, New Delhi.

Prajapat, U. 1999- Details about Terracotta and Symposium. Shaping Earth. University of Wolfhampton and the Architects.

Ranjan, A. and Ranjan, M.P. 2007- Crafts of India, Handmade in India. Ahmedabad National Institute of Design, Published by Council of Handicraft Development Corporations, (COHANDA), New Delhi.

Sankalia, H.D., Deo, S.B. and Ansari, Z.D.. 1969- Excavation at Ahar (Timbavati), Deccan College, Pune.

Sankalia, H.D. 1979- Indian Archaeology Today. Ajanta Publications, Delhi.

Sant, U. 1997- Terracotta Art of Rajasthan (From Pre-Harappan and Harappan Times to the Gupta Periods). Aryan Books International, New Delhi.

Saraswati, B. 1978- Pottery Making Cultures and Indian Civilization. Shakti Malik Abhinav Publications, New Delhi.

Saraswati, B and Behura, N.K.. 1966- Pottery Techniques in Peasant India. Anthropological Survey of India, Govt. Of India, Calcutta 13.

Shinde, V. and Possehl, G.L.. 2005- 'A Report on the Excavations at Gilund, 1999- 2001'. Catherine Jarrige (ed.) South Asian Archaeology, (pp. 293- 302). Paris.

Shinde, V. 2000- 'The Origin and Development of the

Chalcolithic in Central India'. Indo Pacific Prehistory Assiciation Bulletin 19, (Maleka Papers, Vol 3).

Singh, K.S. 1998- People of India: Rajasthan, Part 1. Volume XXXVIII, Anthropological Survey of India. Popular Prakashan Pvt. Ltd., Mumbai.